A STEP-BY-STEP GUIDE TO
GROWING & DISPLAYING
ROSES

A STEP-BY-STEP GUIDE TO

GROWING & DISPLAYING
ROSES

Authors
John Mattock • Jane Newdick
Photographer
Neil Sutherland

WHITECAP BOOKS

3140
This edition published 1993 by Whitecap Books Ltd.
1086 West 3rd Street, North Vancouver, B.C., Canada V7P 3J6
© 1993 CLB Publishing Ltd., Godalming, Surrey, England
Printed and bound in Singapore by Tien Wah Press
ISBN 1-55110-076-2

Edited and designed: Ideas into Print
Photographs: Neil Sutherland
Typesetting: Ideas into Print and Bureau 2000
Production Director: Gerald Hughes
Production: Ruth Arthur, Sally Connolly,
Andrew Whitelaw, Neil Randles

THE AUTHORS

John Mattock has spent a lifetime in horticulture,
principally growing roses and traveling the world to assess
and judge new varieties. He holds the Royal Horticultural
Society's highest award, the Victoria Medal of Honor for
services to Horticulture and is chairman of the committee
that judges floral exhibits at Chelsea and other shows. He
has won 16 Gold Medals at Chelsea for Mattock's Rose
exhibits and is Vice-President of the Royal National Rose
Society, which recently honored him for his contribution to
its work. As an international consultant and acknowledged
expert, he is currently engaged in advising and lecturing on
all aspects of garden design.

Jane Newdick worked for a major international magazine
company before branching out on her own to work from
her home in the countryside. She regularly contributes to a
number of well-known magazines, as well as writing books
on flower arranging and using flowers in a variety of ways
to create unusual and beautiful decorations for the home.

PHOTOGRAPHER

Neil Sutherland has more than 25 years experience in a
wide range of photographic fields, including still-life,
portraiture, reportage, natural history, cookery, landscape
and travel. His work has been published in countless books
and magazines throughout the world.

Half-title page: The superb double blooms of 'Bonica'.
Title page: 'Mme. Isaac Perreire', ringed with scabious and
cornflowers, makes an unusual decoration.
Copyright page: 'Crimson Shower' borders a lily pond.

CONTENTS

Part One - Growing Roses

Part Two - Displaying Roses

Part One

GROWING ROSES

The rose is a native of the temperate zones and thrives best given a cool, frosty winter, a mild spring, sun-filled summer days and a regular supply of water. However, it has also proved to be surprisingly versatile, tolerating a wide range of temperatures and variable amounts of sunlight and rainfall. In fact, as long you avoid exposing roses to conditions of perpetual dry heat or prolonged intense cold, there are few places in the world where you cannot grow them.

Roses are found in a wide variety of colors and forms: wild roses add color to the countryside in early summer, sophisticated blooms grace the bride's wedding bouquet and a wide range of cultivated varieties decorate our gardens. As well as the flowers of the rose, we can enjoy their beautiful, decorative hips in autumn. Roses also vary tremendously in size, from the smallest miniature varieties currently enjoying enormous popularity to the vast ramblers that compete with other plants in the record books. The modern rose has been bred to withstand disease, to flower recurrently and to give pleasure not only as a garden plant, but also as a cut flower, bringing messages of love, hope and comfort. Even the smallest garden or town patio can find room for a rose bush and the largest landscapes are enhanced by the eye-catching splashes of color provided by the world's most popular plant.

In this part of the book we look first at the various types of roses available and then consider all aspects of growing them successfully, with practical information on suitable locations and soils, planting, pruning, seasonal care, diseases and propagation. The section closes with a brief look at preparing roses for showing, a fitting springboard into the second part of the book, which deals with displaying roses in the home.

The blue flowers of love-in-a-mist create a perfect foil for the pastel blooms of the shrub rose 'Ballerina'.

Specie roses

Surprisingly, many of the ancestors of our familiar garden roses are still in existence, often still growing in their natural habitat. These original types are called specie roses, the familiar wild roses that grow in our hedgerows. They include *Rosa virginiana* from North America, the dog rose, *R. canina*, from Europe and *R. chinensis* from the Far East. Specie roses have only ever been discovered in the Northern Hemisphere and of the 120 different identifiable types only 15-20 have ever contributed to the modern rose. We tend to think of the rose as being a development of western culture, but it is a fact that the modern rose would not exist if it had not been for the influx of breeding stock from the Middle and Far East. Many of the wild roses collected from their native habitat now play an important part in enhancing the beauty of our shrub borders. Many varieties have unique characteristics - colored foliage, an abundance of blossom, good plant shapes and a superb harvest of hips. They range in size from just 6in(15cm) to 40ft(12.4m), require very little seasonal maintenance and, in addition, are virtually disease-free.

Right: Rosa xanthina spontanea *'Canary Bird'* is a slightly pendulous shrub that grows to 6ft(1.8m), with many yellow flowers in late spring.

Left: Rosa moyesii *'Geranium'* is a 6ft(1.8m) tall rose that produces bright geranium red, single flowers, followed by bottle-shaped hips in the autumn.

Below: Rosa gallica *'Complicata'* will develop into an enormous sprawling shrub 5ft(1.5m) high and 10ft(3m) across, with single, large flowers.

The rugosa species make superb specimen plants for most gardens. They produce a spectacular harvest of large, tomato-shaped hips that attract birds in the autumn.

Never prune or dead-head these plants. Pruning will result in stunted growth and no hips.

Rugosas will grow to about 5ft(1.5m), are completely disease-resistant and also have a beautiful scent.

A FINE SELECTION OF WILD ROSE SPECIES

R. ecae var. 'Helen Knight'
R. forrestiana
R. gallica 'Complicata'
R. highdownensis
R. macrophylla
R. moyesii 'Geranium'
R. omiensis pteracantha (sericia pteracantha)
R. pomifera (Apple Rose)
R. primula (Incense Rose)
R. roxburghii (Chestnut Rose)
R. glauca (rubrifolia)
R. rugosa alba
R. rugosa rubra
R. soulieana
R. sweginzowii
R. woodsii fendleri

Above: Rosa rugosa 'Scabrosa' is the ideal rose for hedging, with the added bonus of beautiful, globular, red hips in autumn. Rugosas are tolerant of practically any soil and appear proof against most common rose pests.

Left: Rosa omiensis pteracantha. *The large, translucent red thorns on the young growth are a feature of this upright, 10ft(3m)-tall shrub. It has fernlike foliage and small, white, four-petalled flowers. Position it so that the light shines through the thorns.*

13

Old garden roses

Towards the end of the eighteenth century, intrepid plant collectors returned from the Far East with roses that carried the most coveted of genes, the ability to flower more than once each year. These first imports were crossed with their European cousins to produce the direct parents of the modern rose. The early novelties of the 1800s, along with their ancestors, make up that intriguing section in rose catalogs called 'The old garden roses', a title recently updated to 'heritage roses'. Heritage roses are exclusively shrubs that in the main have rather a lax habit and vary in height from 2 to 6ft(60-180cm). These old roses are easy to grow. Their constitution is very strong - indeed they would not be in existence today if it were otherwise - and at the same time, they retain their novelty value. Another interesting feature is that many of the older varieties can produce exciting variations, such as 'Rosa Mundi', 'Baron Girod de l'Ain' and 'Mme. Pierre Oger'. The history and development of the rose is a living spectacle that has given rise to an industry devoted to immortalizing these lovely flowers, whether it be reproducing them for decorative purposes or preserving the real thing.

Left: The large double blooms of Rosa rugosa 'Blanc Double de Coubert' are purest white and heavily scented. The plant has tough, leathery leaves and grows to about 5ft(1.5m). Like most rugosas, it will make a good hedge.

Below: Rosa gallica 'Charles de Mills' is a beautiful old rose with an exciting petal formation. This vigorous plant can grow to about 5ft (1.5m) tall.

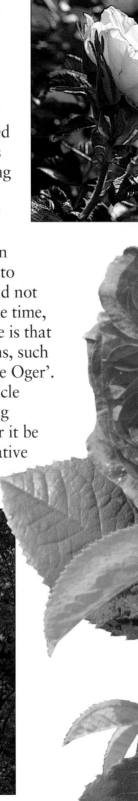

Below: 200 years ago, Rosa 'Fantin-Latour' was a popular cut flower variety. The pale pink, cupped flowers have a beautiful fragrance.

Large, dark green leaves support the purple-red flowers in mid-summer. The weight of the blooms produces swathes of tumbling flowers.

A FINE SELECTION OF OLD GARDEN ROSES

Baron Girod de l'Ain
Blanc Double de Coubert *
Cécile Brünner
Charles de Mills *
Common Moss (Pink) *
Comte de Chambord *
Fantin-Latour *
Ferdinand Pichard
Great Maiden's Blush *
Louise Odier *
Mme. Hardy *
Mme. Isaac Perreire *
Mme. Pierre Oger *
Paul Neyron *
Rosa Mundi (*R. gallica* 'Versicolor') *
Roseraie de l'Hay *
Souvenir du Dr Jamain *
Variegata di Bologna *
William Lobb (Old Velvet Moss)
Zéphirine Drouhin *

*Fragrant flowers

Above: *Lovely Rosa bourboniana 'Louise Odier' has large incurved double blooms of rose-pink shaded lilac, with a pleasant fragrance. The plant has an arching habit and grows to 48in(120cm).*

Below: *Rosa gallica 'Versicolor' ('Rosa Mundi') is probably the oldest heritage rose commonly grown today. In early summer, masses of striped blooms appear on a relatively short plant about 36in(90cm) tall.*

Once blooms are past their best, dead-head them heavily to encourage strong new growth.

The gallicas flower only once, but the blooms last for a long time and can be used to create stunning floral art decorations.

Hybrid tea bush roses

Once the color begins to fade, dead-head the rose, removing old blooms to allow new branches to develop.

The legendary hybrid tea rose has classically shaped blooms, is easy to grow and the most recent introductions are very tough and relatively disease-free. All hybrid teas produce large blooms throughout the summer. The first hybrid teas were inevitably limited in color range, but in this century breeders have successfully introduced the most vivid yellows, startling vermilions, a host of blends and bicolors, blues and now grays, greens and stripes. Many famous examples are household names. 'Peace' - appropriately named in 1946 after World War Two - is famous for its wondrous growth and perfection of bloom, 'Tropicana' ('Super Star') is an extraordinary vermilion and the more recent 'Silver Jubilee' is a subtle blend of pinks and boasts a high flower rate. The majority of hybrid teas are cultivated in individual rose beds, either singly or in groups of color or variety. To encourage them to give of their best, make sure you prepare the soil well, prune them every year in spring and give them an occasional feed. All are hardy and thrive in normal temperate climates. Like all types of rose they will benefit from full sunlight, but semi-shade is not impossible.

Right: *'Blessings' could well be described as the perfect hybrid tea rose. It is a beautiful coral salmon color, with fragrant blooms and an even growth that will fill a bed and provide abundant flower throughout the summer and autumn. The even, deep green foliage is very hardy and disease-resistant, a perfect foil for the bloom.*

This bloom will look good for another three or four days.

The foliage of a good bedding rose is as important as the flower.

16

Left: *Although 'Peace' is an old rose by modern standards, it remains very popular and deserves its reputation as the most famous rose ever bred. It will make a large shrub if lightly pruned.*

Right: *'Tequila Sunrise' is one of the most exciting new roses recently introduced. The spectacular, deep yellow blooms are heavily edged in vivid scarlet and retain their color for a long time.*

Below: *Large-flowered roses, such as 'Heart Throb' ('Paul Shirville') shown here, are just as attractive when all the blooms are full out. The peach-shaded, salmon pink flowers on a plant of medium height have a delightful fragrance.*

For decorative purposes, cut the rose at this stage and enjoy its beauty as it opens.

A SELECTION OF FRAGRANT HYBRID TEA ROSES

Alec's Red
Blessings
Fragrant Cloud
Fragrant Hour
Keepsake
Loving Memory
Heart Throb (Paul Shirville)
Fragrant Charm 84
(Royal William)
Solitaire
Troika

A SELECTION OF LARGE-FLOWERED HYBRID TEA ROSES

Freedom
Ingrid Bergman
Just Joey
Loving Memory
Pascali
Peace
Savoy Hotel
Silver Jubilee
Rock-n-Roll (Tango)
Tequila Sunrise

Right: *'Just Joey's' coppery orange blooms have a unique coloring. Acclaimed as a breakthrough on account of its novel petal formation, this rose has earned many awards. It flowers early and will grow in the most uncompromising soils. An application of fertilizer in midsummer encourages beautiful autumn color.*

Floribunda bush roses

By definition, a floribunda bush rose is any variety that bears clusters or sprays of flowers. Because of its checkered history and development, this group has been known by several names, including *hybrid polyanthas*, Poulsen roses and grandifloras. Although 'cluster-flowered' is the newest and probably most accurate description, the most commonly accepted term remains floribunda. Essentially, hybrid teas and floribundas are both bush roses requiring identical care. Where they do differ is in their flower potential. A hybrid tea is a large bloom borne singly on a stem, whereas a floribunda is a cluster of blooms, no single flower being dominant or larger than any other. There is the added bonus that a cluster provides a longer flowering period.

Take care when selecting floribundas as they can vary tremendously in height. Although there is some variation in hybrid teas, the differences are not so obvious, but certain varieties of floribunda can grow as much as 36in(90cm) taller than others. At one time, floribundas were said to be tougher than hybrid teas, but today all roses are more resilient. Like hybrid teas, floribundas are ideal for formal beds, although they will grow virtually anywhere, provided they are maintained properly. When grown in groups they can lend color to a dull shrub border and their color range is equal to any other type of rose. To ensure a continuity of flower, be sure to dead-head immediately after the first flush of flower. A midsummer feed is essential. (See *Seasonal maintenance* on pages 56-57)

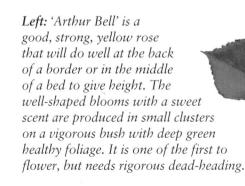

Left: 'Arthur Bell' is a good, strong, yellow rose that will do well at the back of a border or in the middle of a bed to give height. The well-shaped blooms with a sweet scent are produced in small clusters on a vigorous bush with deep green healthy foliage. It is one of the first to flower, but needs rigorous dead-heading.

Left: 'Margaret Merrill' has exceptionally large flowers for a floribunda rose, white with a hint of blush. The very sweetly scented plants are of medium height, with deep green, large, leathery foliage. An ideal variety that fills a bed to perfection.

'Memento' dies prettily, which is a bonus when large heads are difficult to dead-head.

Left: 'English Miss' is a pretty blush that blends well in color schemes without clashing with some of the more strident colors. The plant is of medium height, with handsome mid-green foliage and flowers early in the season with a pleasing fragrance.

A FINE SELECTION OF FLORIBUNDA BUSH ROSES

Amber Queen *
Dicky (Anisley Dickson)
Anna Livia
Arthur Bell *
English Miss *
Fragrant Delight *
Hannah Gordon
Harvest Fayre *
Iceberg
Sunsprite (Korresia) *
Margaret Merrill *
Memento
Scented Air *
Shocking Blue *
Southampton *
The Times Rose
Trumpeter

*Fragrant flowers

Left: Because of its continuity, 'Memento' has been compared with 'Iceberg'. The large clusters of salmon-vermilion, medium-sized blooms are a feast of color all summer, growing on an average-sized bush with strong healthy foliage about 36in(90cm) tall.

The secret of a good floribunda is the constant renewal of young growth, graphically illustrated here.

Take care when positioning roses of this color; pinks can clash violently.

Modern shrub roses

What is a modern shrub rose? Strictly speaking, all roses are shrubs, but the modern conventional hybrid tea or floribunda has come to be accepted as a bush, while the more prolific and bigger plant is designated a shrub. For practical purposes, we could say that a modern shrub is a floribunda trimmed to shape and not cut down hard every spring. Although many people assume that a modern rose is by definition repeat flowering, this is not necessarily true of all the varieties in this group. The majority produce magnificent splashes of color in high summer, followed by a small flush in the autumn. They respond well to extra rose fertilizer applied as soon as the summer flush has finished to goad them into another display in autumn. They also benefit from heavy dead-heading. Modern shrub roses play a most important part in the design of mixed flowering shrub borders, providing color when most other flowering plants have finished for the season. Very few varieties will make a splash when planted singly; the finest effects are achieved by planting them in threes or fives. Whatever the plan, make sure that the plants have plenty of light, particularly in the spring. Do not be tempted to plant early flowering bulbs at the base of the shrub roses, as this impedes their cultivation and feeding.

Shrub roses respond to heavy dead-heading immediately after the first flush of flower to encourage bloom in the autumn.

'English Roses' vary in height and garden worthiness, but make adaptable shrubs.

Right: 'Ballerina' is a prolific shrub that grows to 48in (120cm) tall and wide. Its seemingly continuous sprays of bloom are reminiscent of phlox.

A FINE SELECTION OF MODERN SHRUB ROSES

Ballerina
Buff Beauty *
Cerise Bouquet
Felicia *
Frühlingsgold *
Golden Wings
Graham Thomas *
Kordes' Robusta
Lichtkönigen Lucia
Nevada

*Fragrant flowers

Left: 'Frühlingsgold' is one of a small family of modern shrubs with the prefix 'Frühling', meaning spring. These vigorous plants appear to thrive on neglect. The large, pale yellow, single blooms have a wild rose scent.

Always allow 'Graham Thomas' to grow naturally. Do not stake the plant unless it is absolutely necessary - the result is unattractive to look at.

'English Roses' are the result of hybridizing modern HT bush roses with some of the old garden roses, thus combining the recurrent flowering characteristics of the modern rose with the flower formation of the older types.

Above: No other shrub rose can grow to 8-10ft(2.5-3m) high and wide and flower as profusely as this 'Marguerite Hilling'. It requires no pruning and produces a modest second crop of large, single, flushed pink flowers in autumn. It has an equally spectacular creamy white sister, 'Nevada'.

Left: 'Graham Thomas' is a truly magnificent yellow shrub rose with an appealing scent. It is the best - and certainly the healthiest - of the new 'English Roses' and can be expected to attain a height of 48in(120cm).

21

Climbers and ramblers

Until 1800, cultivated roses were a mixture of shrubs and bushes and it was not until new plant forms were introduced from the Far East that it was possible to grow roses to equal the vigor of climbers in other families of flowering plants. The rapid expansion of climbing roses produced a vast range of varieties, many still familiar today. The old ramblers, such as 'Dorothy Perkins', 'Paul's Scarlet' and 'American Pillar', vied for popularity with the climbers - 'Spanish Beauty' ('Mme. Grégoire Staechelin'), 'Mme. Alfred Carrière' and 'Climbing Mrs Sam McGredy' - all of which leads to the question, 'What is the difference between a climber and a rambler?' The short answer is that a rambler has pliable stems and is happier on a fence or trellis that will provide ample support, whereas the wood of a climber is stouter and more suitable for a wall, which offers less support. At one time, with one or two exceptions, ramblers and climbers only flowered once a year, but modern varieties can produce as much bloom in the autumn as in high summer. Today, climbers and ramblers are cataloged as summer-flowering, recurrent-flowering, etc., but most modern recurrent flowering climbers do not have the same vigor as their ancestors.

CLIMBING AND RAMBLING ROSES

Into trees
Albertine *
Bobbie James
Cécile Brünner (climbing)
Paul's Scarlet
Rosa filipes 'Kiftsgate' *
The Garland
Wedding Day

*Fragrant flowers

CLIMBING AND RAMBLING ROSES

Pillar roses
Aloha *
Bantry Bay
Dublin Bay
Golden Showers *
Handel
Laura Ford
Warm Welcome
White Cockade

North and East facing aspects
Spectacular (Danse de Feu)
Dortmund
Gloire de Dijon *
Maigold *
Mermaid
Mme. Alfred Carrière *
The New Dawn *
Zéphirine Drouhin *

*Fragrant flowers

Right: Rosa filipes 'Kiftsgate' can grow through trees to 15ft(4.5m). The creamy scented flowers are followed by many small, round, bright red hips.

Below: Select appropriate varieties with care. 'Golden Showers' is almost perpetually in bloom, but do not expect it to climb through trees.

Above: 'Bantry Bay' is an ideal climber for the small garden. Good-quality blooms flourish on a plant that is easy to control, growing to about 10ft(3m).

Right: 'Sympathie' is a vigorous plant with deep bronze foliage and scarlet crimson flowers during summer and autumn.

CLIMBING AND RAMBLING ROSES

Walls
Climbing Iceberg
Dreaming Spires *
Guinea
Mme. Alfred Carrière *
Maigold *
Mermaid
Parade
Summer Wine *

Fences
Compassion *
Spectacular (Danse de Feu)
Dortmund
Félicité et Perpétue
Grand Hotel
Malaga *
Sympathie

*Fragrant flowers

Standard roses

The standard, or tree, rose became very popular about 100 years ago. Until then, roses were either grown on their own roots (from cuttings) or from seed. Once it was discovered that a superior product could be produced from propagating on a rootstock, it was a short step to producing plants on an elongated stem, however artificial they looked. After a decline in popularity, standard roses are back in fashion, the quality of the stock has improved and gardeners like the height they can add to an otherwise flat-looking rose bed. Choose standard varieties with care; not every bush rose will make a good standard, which should be vigorous but bushy. Many of the newer shrub roses and even ground cover varieties produce admirable heads. Take care when positioning standard roses, as they cannot tolerate windy conditions. In any case, always stake the plants securely. If you are using a standard to add height to a rose bed, consider the vigor of the bedding variety growing beneath the standard. Some bedding roses grow too tall and will overwhelm a good standard.

With careful dead-heading, this beautiful pink and ivory variety will contribute to the beauty of your garden for a long period during the summer and autumn.

Left: *'Peer Gynt' is a good yellow rose with an iron constitution that will produce high-quality blooms. As the petals age, they assume a bright red flush. A well-grown head carries large clusters of perfectly shaped flowers.*

Right: *'Hannah Gordon' is a popular floribunda that will also excel as a standard. Its pleasing distribution of foliage and flower is an asset in any garden. With light pruning, it will eventually grow into a massive plant.*

Left: 'Iceberg' is probably the most recurrent-flowering floribunda and will amply repay a good feeding program. With light pruning, it will develop a very large standard head.

Below: 'Félicité et Perpétue', a classic example of a rambler budded onto a stem, makes a very good weeping standard. Cut out old flowering wood, but allow the plant to grow naturally.

Below: 'Nozomi' is one of many ground cover roses that will produce the most beautiful heads. This spectacular standard requires little or no pruning, yet will develop in a very pleasing manner, with swathes of blooms about 36in(90cm) long.

A FINE SELECTION OF STANDARD ROSES

Hybrid tea and floribunda
Anna Livia
Blessings
Iceberg
Keepsake
Loving Memory
Peace
Silver Jubilee
Trumpeter

Shrub
Ballerina
Canary Bird
Kent
Nozomi
Snow Carpet
Surrey
The Fairy

Weeping
Albéric Barbier
Crimson Shower
Dorothy Perkins
Francois Juranville

Patio and miniature roses

Until recently, rose producers and gardeners accepted that the typical modern rose should be a statuesque plant topped off with the perfect bloom. However, since many rose varieties are simply not suitable for the small garden, the idea emerged of designing a low-growing rose that retained the flower form of the modern bush but was suitable for a small patio or yard. The result was the patio rose, an easy to control, short-growing floribunda bearing conventionally shaped, but tiny blooms. Even smaller than the patio rose, the true miniature rose is happier in a pot or grown as a forcing variety for the pot rose market. Both patio and miniature roses will thrive in the modern garden. However, just because they are small do not be tempted to plant them in rockeries or on alpine slopes, where they will surely die. They are true roses and require the same cultivation as any of the larger varieties.

Allow plenty of room for the roots and feed every spring.

Left: 'Baby Masquerade' grows about 12in(30cm) high. The flowers turn from yellow to red as they age. Dead-head for autumn flower.

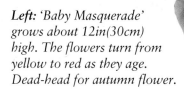

Left: 'The Queen Mother Rose' is an ideal plant for the small garden. The beautifully rounded plants, about 18in(45cm) high, will produce a feast of pure soft pink flowers with a pleasing fragrance. They continue from midsummer until autumn.

Below: 'Sweet Sunblaze' ('Pretty Polly') could be described as designer made for the pot. This reliable patio rose has clear pink blooms almost 2in(5cm) across that produce a veritable blaze of color.

A FINE SELECTION OF PATIO ROSES

Anna Ford
Gentle Touch
Little Bo Peep
Brass Ring (Peek a Boo)
Perestroika
The Queen Mother Rose
Buffalo Bill/Young
Mistress (Regensberg)
St. Boniface
Sweet Dream
Sweet Magic

Above: 'Little Artist' is a complete novelty among the miniature roses. The scarlet blooms with a white eye are exciting to grow. They are easily grown from cuttings and will flower throughout the summer.

This reliable, healthy plant flowers a little later than most patio roses. If lightly pruned, it develops into a small shrub. Growth is laxer than in other patio roses.

Left: Remember to repot miniature roses every year. For best results, grow the plants in clay pots, where the roots are much happier and remain cooler. The plants will also be healthier and produce more flower.

Ground cover roses

In response to the demand for roses to provide color on difficult slopes, road verges, grassy banks and in other informal planting schemes, breeders have developed prostrate or semi-prostrate plants that need little or no maintenance, no pruning, and that provide a lengthy flowering period and great resistance to disease. At first, the color range was limited to pinks and whites, followed by good reds, while the yellow varieties proved a little more difficult to develop. The first varieties were large, sprawling plants that flowered once, but patient development has resulted in recurrent flowering ground cover roses in a full color range, compact enough even for the smallest garden. Take care to choose the correct variety for a specific location, however, and be sure to differentiate between the sometimes enormous varieties, such as 'Red Max Graf' or 'Pheasant', and the more restrained growth of 'Suffolk' and 'Snow Carpet'. Ground cover roses appreciate as much light as possible and like to have their roots in fertile soil. They will grow in semi-shade, but do not expect so much flower. They will provide cover and color in the most hostile situations, as well as helping to keep the weeds at bay.

A FINE SELECTION OF GROUND COVER ROSES

For the big garden
Ferdy
Grouse
Pheasant
Pink Bells
Red Max Graf
White Bells
White Max Graf

For the small garden
Flower Carpet
Kent
Northamptonshire
Nozomi
Snow Carpet
Suffolk
Surrey
The Fairy

Most modern ground cover roses will grow from cuttings (see page 66). They require only the minimum of pruning.

'Essex' has small, pretty pink flowers and disease-resistant foliage.

Right: *The 'County' series of ground cover roses provide color and green foliage in many difficult situations. 'Essex' is ideal for the small garden and flowers all through the summer.*

Left: Rosa 'Bonica' is a popular environmental plant, widely grown in the USA. Sprays of pastel pink, small double blooms are produced from midsummer until autumn and cover banks and 'green' areas.

Right: 'Suffolk' will cover an average area of about 11ft²(1m²). It will grow little taller than 12in(30cm). Clusters of bright scarlet flowers persist from midsummer to the late autumn.

Below: 'Grouse' is the first of the new generation of ground cover roses. It is capable of growing 8-10ft(2.5-3m) in a season. In midsummer it is covered with heavily scented, small, very pale pink flowers.

Never prune this type of rose. Allow it to grow naturally and accumulate a 'cushion' of foliage.

29

Choosing a good plant

A rose tree takes two years to produce. It must be lifted, graded, stored and is eventually despatched as a bare root plant between autumn and spring. Alternatively, it is root-wrapped for sale off the shelf or containerized (potted) for sale in the spring or summer. Problems can arise during this process, but a top-quality plant is easy to recognize. It must have a good root system, free of torn or damaged material, and the top growth - even if it is pruned - must have substantial wood and the strength to bear healthy growth and flower. Damage is most likely to occur during storage. If plants are allowed to dry out, the wood will shrivel. Spindly growth may indicate that the rose is old or the compost is poor. Root-wrapped plants are probably at greatest risk. If they are stored in poor conditions and kept on the shelf too long, the result is forced green growth and a short life. When buying a containerized plant, make sure it is well established. Buying a potted rose too early in the season can result in fatal damage to the root system.

Below: 'Ballerina' is an extremely popular shrub rose for planting in a mixed border, where it will provide superb color over a long flowering season.

BAD PLANT

This growth should have been cut back hard to encourage strong wood.

This is typical of the poorest type of containerized rose plant. It was probably potted on too late and offered for sale the following spring.

You can always identify an old plant by the color of the wood. A fresh and healthy plant is a bright deep green.

A rose in a pot of this size will live about six months. After this time, it is difficult to maintain and prone to disease.

GOOD PLANT

By its very nature, a rose bush is not the ideal subject for containerization. Given a good-quality compost, the roots will grow very quickly and soon fill out the pot. Look for good strong growth and make sure that the foliage is free of disease and the plant is well watered.

Shoots are very tender at this stage and easily damaged, which will retard progress by some weeks.

This view shows the root system filling the pot well. If the roots look brown and old, the plant has probably been potted too long.

BAD PLANT

Sometimes the stock onto which the rose is budded produces extraneous growths called suckers, which should have been removed.

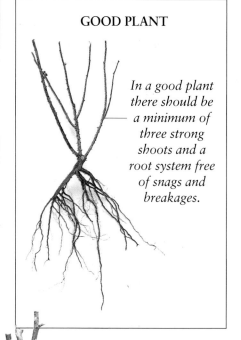

GOOD PLANT

In a good plant there should be a minimum of three strong shoots and a root system free of snags and breakages.

BAD PLANT

GOOD PLANT

This plant has been on the shelf too long and is beginning to make growth. Buy your stock from reputable outlets that store plants correctly.

This is a well-cared for plant. Cut this tie after planting.

Plant the rose so that the soil reaches this level. There should be no scars below this point revealing old sucker traces.

The wrapping keeps the plant moist. Do not allow it to dry out after purchase.

Choosing the best location

Even in the most difficult growing situations, the rose plant will give great satisfaction, but given ideal conditions it is superb. So what are the ideal conditions? Primarily, roses appreciate a location in full sunlight and out of cold drafts. Drafts often whistle between buildings, flow from nearby cold woods or rattle through a gap in the hedge; roses planted in these situations will not thrive. It may not always be possible to plant roses in positions that receive full sunlight and semi-shade is often acceptable, particularly for the new ground cover varieties. However, some situations are impossible - for example, a continually sunless wall with no reflected light. Roses need water, so avoid planting them in a dry position, such as a rockery. It is tempting to try and grow miniature roses in rockeries, but they simply will not survive for long in such a position. Remember that standard roses need adequate staking and are not really suitable for very open windy positions. Slow-growing climbers and ramblers are suitable for covering a wall in a small garden, whereas vigorous rambling plants do best growing around large arbors and pergolas. Make sure that all roses receive the maximum amount of light in spring and do not allow heavy-leaved plants, such as tulips, to grow too close to the base of the bushes Also, avoid smothering the base with dense creeping ground cover plants.

Encourage a good spread of bloom by careful dead-heading and eliminating old woody growth. Tie in the new wood as it develops.

***Above:** A good, vigorous rambler requires the maximum amount of support. A pergola or fence is ideal for this 'Félicité et Perpétue' to grow and be seen to its best advantage.*

***Left:** 'Bantry Bay' is a typical modern recurrent climber that thrives in full sunlight. It will provide a display of bloom throughout the season if well fed and tied to good supports.*

Take care to plant a climber well away from the doorway to prevent damage to both plant and passing visitors.

Left: *Carefully mark out the planting positions of the roses before ordering them. The general rule is to allow 24in(60cm) between one bush and another for beautiful, well-grown plants with plenty of growing space.*

Below: *Here the vigorous rambler 'Albertine', the slow-growing climber 'Pink Perpétue' and the shrub rose 'Ballerina' complement each other superbly and provide glorious color over a very long flowering period.*

Below: *The hybrid tea 'Rosemary Harkness' is typical of the many roses that will thrive almost anywhere, but whose flower potential is determined by the amount of light they receive.*

Here, the roses benefit dramatically from full sun. Do not forget the midsummer feed to maintain this strong growth and good color.

Roses planted on the shady side of the bed are clearly at a disadvantage.

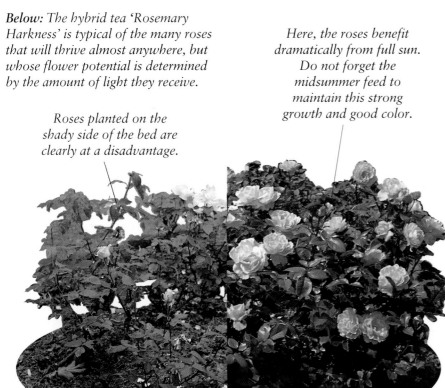

33

Making the best of your soil

The rose is a very tolerant plant that will thrive in most soils. However, it does have some essential requirements and the first of these is good drainage, which means that surplus water in the soil should drain away efficiently. Winter flooding does not appear to be detrimental, but continuously boggy conditions are no good at all. If you cannot improve such conditions then you will have disappointing results trying to grow roses. Soils can vary from the lightest sand to the heaviest clay and from alkaline chalky soils to acidic peaty ones. Chalky soils are not particularly good for growing roses, but you can improve them by adding peat or peat substitute and feeding the plants with a foliar feed, but this can be very expensive. Sandy soils are easier to handle, but are sometimes described as 'hungry' because they absorb organic material very quickly. The remedy is to build up the food availability with copious amounts of well-rotted compost or farmyard manure. Heavy soils have a reputation for producing the best roses, but this is largely a fallacy. They need breaking up with organic material and sand to avoid becoming waterlogged. The ideal soil for cultivating roses is a well-drained, deep loam. If you are not sure about the type of soil in your garden, try observing your neighbor's land and seeing which plants grow successfully there. Do remember that you cannot successfully replant an old rose bed with new roses until the bed has had a rest period - usually for about three years. Alternatively, replace all the old soil.

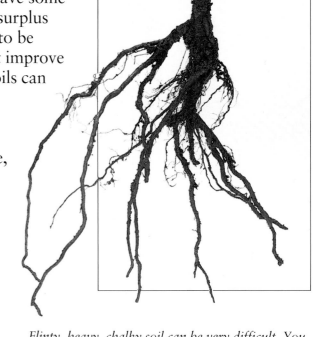

Below: The rose has a tremendous root system that can grow very long, but it is the small fibrous roots that provide the plant with its food.

Flinty, heavy, chalky soil can be very difficult. You can help roses to thrive by adding a mixture based on peat or peat substitute around the roots when planting them and giving plants a regular foliar feed.

Right: A sandy soil will give good results if you incorporate plenty of organic manure into it. It has the advantage of always being well drained and produces the earliest flowers in the garden.

This type of soil will support many of the wild, or specie, roses that can give amazing crops of decorative hips in autumn.

Below: *There are several test kits that you can use to register the acidity or alkalinity of your soil. The ideal pH level is 6.5, which is slightly acid.*

Follow the instructions carefully, collecting the soil you wish to test from about 9in(23cm) below the surface.

Chopped bark is a suitable top dressing and subdues weeds. Remember to give the plants a feed, as there is no food value in raw bark.

Good-quality sharp sand helps to break up heavy clay soil, aids drainage and makes it easier for the fibrous roots to take up food.

Adding ground limestone is the most appropriate method of correcting a very acid soil. Spreading about 2oz per square yard (70gm/m²) every two years will give good results.

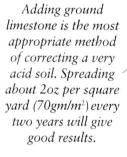

A deep, loamy, well-drained soil must be every rose grower's dream. Avoid handling it in wet conditions; its structure may be destroyed, causing problems when dry weather returns.

Heavy clay soil is reputed to produce the best-quality rose blooms, but it is very hard work for the gardener. This type of soil improves if it is subjected to frost after early autumn cultivation. Adding generous quantities of organic material will also help to produce a more open soil and encourage a good root system to develop.

Planting a bush rose

You can plant bush roses in two forms - bare-rooted or containerized. In either case, prepare the ground by digging over the soil and incorporating well-rotted garden compost or farmyard manure into the top layer. In many soils, this is only possible when the earth is friable; never handle soil when it is waterlogged. If possible, break up the subsoil below the cultivated top layer. Use a suitable planting mixture around the roots. Bare-rooted rose plants are available from autumn to early spring. If the plants are dry, soak them in a bucket of water for about two hours and then plant them out straight away. If conditions are not suitable for planting, heel the plants in as described on page 40, but never handle the plants in a frozen condition. For the best results, plant bare-rooted roses in the autumn. Although containerized plants are available all the year round, the best time to plant them is late spring or early summer. The very nature of the root system of a containerized rose does not lend itself to mishandling, so avoid disturbing the root ball when taking the plant out of the container.

1 *Prepare a hole 12in(30cm) across and deep, with a stick in the corner. Place the plant against the stick, allowing a free run of the roots.*

Planting a containerized bush rose

Avoid damaging this well-developed network of fine feeding roots.

1 *Today, most roses are containerized in a rigid pot, which makes extracting them simple. A good sharp tap will allow the plant to drop out without root damage.*

2 *Place the plant in the prepared hole approximately 12in(30cm) across and deep. Add a spadeful of planting mixture around the roots. Avoid damage to roots or foliage.*

3 *Fill in the hole with a planting mixture. Either buy this from a garden shop or prepare it by mixing a handful of bonemeal in a large bucket of moist peat or peat substitute.*

2 *The junction of the root system and the wood of the tree should be at surface level. Add a good spadeful of planting mixture to cover the roots.*

3 *Fill the rest of the hole with soil, making sure that any manure added in the course of preparing the site does not touch the plant's roots.*

4 *Ideally, firm in the soil thoroughly around the roots. If conditions are unfavorable, wait until the soil is dry or in a more friable state.*

4 *Make sure the plant is securely anchored. Be sure to water it with about a gallon of water and maintain this level of watering on a weekly basis until it is well established.*

Right: *'Loving Memory' ('Burgund '81') has the classic form of a modern HT bush rose, with fragrant blooms and dark green foliage.*

Planting climbers and ramblers

Ideally, planting roses is a job for the autumn or winter although, of course, you can plant containerized roses in the late spring or early summer. With climbers or ramblers the planting season is the same, but establishing the correct planting position and selecting the appropriate variety is of paramount importance. If the rose is to grow against a wall

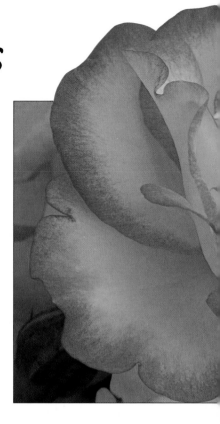

Right: 'Handel' is a stunning climber that grows to about 10ft(3m) and is ideal for the smaller garden. Creamy white blooms suffused with a bright rose edge to the petals grow on long stems, which make it good for cutting.

or in a restricted space, a moderate climber is ideal. Against a fence you will require something a little more vigorous, while a pergola will accommodate most types of climber or rambler. If you want the rose to grow into a tree, there are many fast-growing varieties. A particular problem may arise when planting in a new garden where builders have been working. You may well find an accumulation of old cement and rubble, particularly at the bottom of walls, so before planting, remove 3-4 cubic feet(about 0.1m³) of waste material from each planting position and replace this with prepared compost or soil. Incorporate well-rotted manure or garden waste - about one forkful per cubic foot. Prepare the plant support (see the panel on using a vine eye, page 39) and build posts or pergolas in position before planting the rose.

1 Prepare a planting hole measuring about 12in(30cm) across and deep. If available, work a forkful of well-rotted compost into the soil below the plant, but not touching the roots.

2 Position the rose. Add a bucket of planting mixture around the roots. Use peat or peat substitute, mixed with a handful of bonemeal or a ready made mixture. Fill the hole with soil.

3 New climbers and ramblers have normally been trimmed down to 24in(60cm) before delivery. Cut the restraining string. Make sure the soil around the roots is well firmed in.

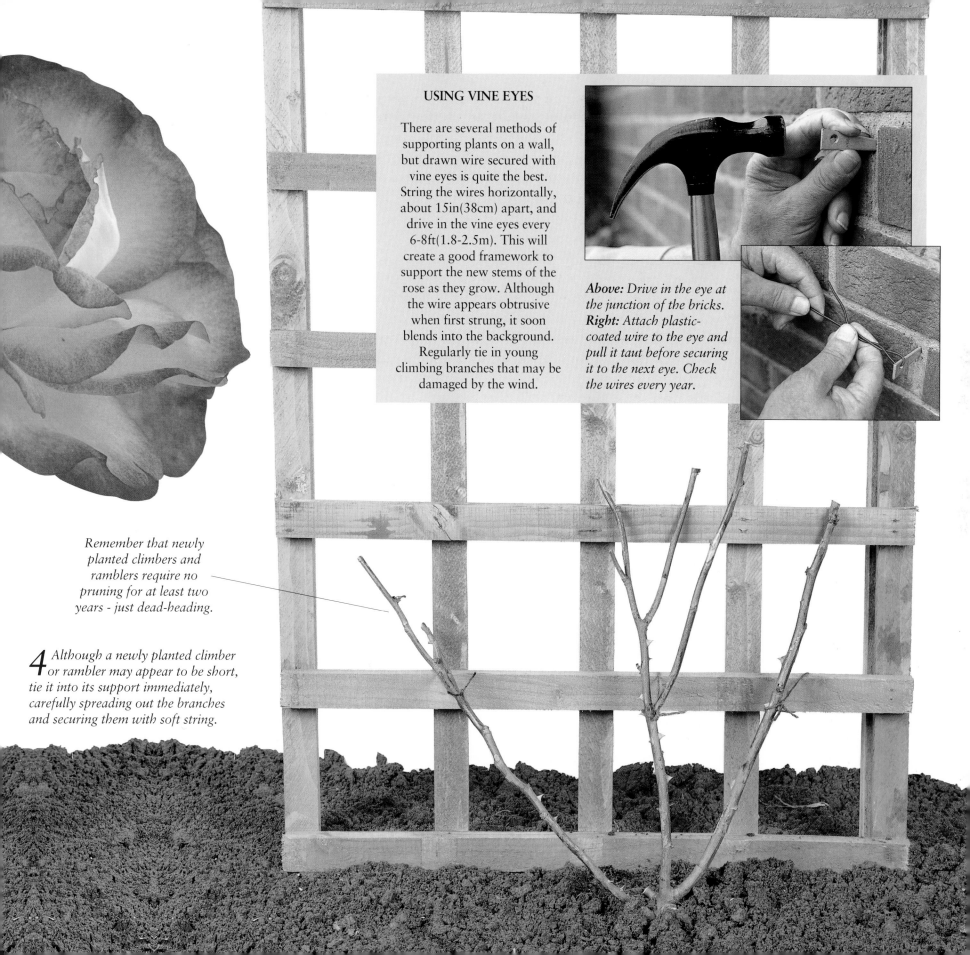

USING VINE EYES

There are several methods of supporting plants on a wall, but drawn wire secured with vine eyes is quite the best. String the wires horizontally, about 15in(38cm) apart, and drive in the vine eyes every 6-8ft(1.8-2.5m). This will create a good framework to support the new stems of the rose as they grow. Although the wire appears obtrusive when first strung, it soon blends into the background. Regularly tie in young climbing branches that may be damaged by the wind.

Above: *Drive in the eye at the junction of the bricks.*
Right: *Attach plastic-coated wire to the eye and pull it taut before securing it to the next eye. Check the wires every year.*

Remember that newly planted climbers and ramblers require no pruning for at least two years - just dead-heading.

4 *Although a newly planted climber or rambler may appear to be short, tie it into its support immediately, carefully spreading out the branches and securing them with soft string.*

Planting a standard rose

A standard is the most expensive rose plant you will ever buy, so take the greatest care when deciding where to plant it. Choose a position that offers the best protection from the wind and stake it securely so that it quickly becomes established and grows on strongly. There is nothing more heart-breaking than losing a standard rose through wind damage, so check all stakes at least twice a year. Remember, a new stake is cheaper than a new plant. Never allow the plant roots to dry out. As a precaution, heel the roses in as soon as you bring them back from the nursery. To do this, simply dig a shallow trench and lay the plant at an angle of 45° so that the roots are in the trench. Then cover the roots with loose soil. This will keep the plant in good condition while you prepare the main planting hole. If necessary, dip the roots in water first. In any case, they will certainly benefit from being dipped just before they are planted. This does not mean watering them once they are in the ground, although this might be helpful in a very dry season. Do not plant standards in freezing conditions. No plant responds well to being handled in a frozen state, particularly standard roses.

The plant may appear top heavy at this stage. If it has arrived from the nursery untrimmed, cut the branches back, leaving about 12in(30cm) growth on the tree.

A strong stake is essential for a new plant with a thin stem. The stem will thicken up as it ages.

1 *Choose a firm stake made of straight-grained, knot-free wood. Knots cause poles to snap. Drive the stake in after digging the hole, but before positioning the plant. Put the stake on the side facing the prevailing wind.*

2 *Because the roots of a standard are larger than those of a bush rose, make the planting hole correspondingly larger. Spread roots out evenly in the planting hole.*

3 *Offer up the rose to ensure it is in the right position. Make sure the junction of the root and stem is level with the top of the soil. If planted any deeper, growth will be stunted and if planted any shallower, the roots are at risk from drying out.*

4 Never use a stake that has recently been painted with wood preservative, as this may contain a weedkiller or other chemicals that harm plants.

When firmly anchored, the top of the stake should reach to just below the first shoot.

Use a good-quality strap to secure the rose to the stake. Never use plastic twine, which is abrasive and can cause considerable damage to the stem. Adjust the tie as the stem thickens.

Below: *Floribundas make very good heads if you grow the correct variety. 'Memento', shown here, is one of the best and will flower for a long time throughout the summer and autumn.*

5 Cover the roots entirely with a good planting mixture or mix your own, using one bucket of peat or peat substitute to a handful of bonemeal.

6 Tread the soil in firmly around the roots to help them become established. This may not be possible in wet weather, but is essential before the tree starts to grow in the spring.

Basic pruning techniques

Many myths have arisen about the cultivation of roses. The need to prune them has meant that many new gardeners have been dissuaded from growing the world's most popular flower because of a fear that they cannot cope with 'the pruning'. It is encouraging to learn that the average rose plant is a very tough individual that will withstand a tremendous amount of abuse and neglect, but also responds well to some very elementary management. In fact, by the very nature of its breeding, a modern rose plant needs to be controlled if it is going to provide the finest display in the garden. Pruning simply means reducing the plant seasonally so that it makes new growth and bears superior bloom. In the early spring the process is called pruning, in the summer, dead-heading, and in autumn, cutting back to face the winter. It is vital to prevent a rose plant expending its energy on maintaining old wood that has fulfilled its function and that will only harbor disease. A golden rule is never to cut a rose plant when the wood is in a frozen condition or during a hot dry spell. And remember that specie roses and the majority of the old garden roses do not require the same harsh treatment as the sophisticated modern hybrids.

Left: Efficient pruning in the spring has given this shrub rose, 'Golden Wings', a good shape at the height of the growing season. This is the plant shown being pruned on pages 46-47.

PRUNING A MAIDEN BUSH

A young rose bush newly planted in the autumn will need pruning in the spring of its first year. Cut the plant back to about 5in(13cm) above the ground. It is likely that the soil around the rose will have been loosened by winter frosts, so it is a good idea to firm it down again in the spring when you prune the rose back. Remember that newly planted roses do not need feeding during their first growing season.

WHERE TO MAKE THE CUT

This cut has been made far too close to the bud. Once the bud has grown, it will blow out in the wind due to lack of adequate support.

In this example, the length of wood left on the branch above the bud is far too long. The stem will 'die back' and harbor disease spores.

Left: *A well-pruned climber or rambler will provide beauty and grace even in the winter months. The most vigorous stems have been arched into a horizontal position to induce a profusion of flowering growths.*

Above: *Autumn is the best season to remove old branches, as dead wood is much easier to identify at this time. Sharp long arms, or 'parrot bills', as shown here, are ideal for the task.*

Below: *You will need a much stronger implement to remove the larger stems. The pruning saw being used here will remove the largest branches and very good designs are now available. If you can get close to the base of the plant, hold the stem as you saw through it.*

Strong gloves are essential. Thorns can cause nasty injuries.

Side-by-side secateurs produce a clean cut, are easy to maintain and stay sharp.

Above: *Most branches can be cut back with a sharp pair of secateurs, but never attempt to cut dead wood with these, as it will ruin the cutting edge, with very costly consequences.*

A jagged cut means that your secateurs are not sharp. Damaged wood will create a haven for small insects and other creatures.

This is the ideal length to aim for when pruning. The slanted cut will soon heal up and the bud will develop into a strong branch.

Pruning a wild or specie rose

Below: Rosa gallica 'Complicata' will make a big rambling shrub not unlike an enormous blackberry bush. The beautiful large, single, pink flowers with golden centers smother the plant in midsummer.

By definition, a wild rose is a specie that has existed for hundreds of years and flourished without any outside help. In the wild, ageing branches occasionally die back and subsequently rot away. In the garden, you can assist this process by completely removing the offending branches. Most wild roses will grow in a garden environment without any form of control. By their nature, the majority will flower only once in the season, followed by hips in the autumn. Therefore, there are two golden rules: never shorten good, well-grown stems, since the branches must be allowed to grow naturally, and never dead-head or you will not get hips in the autumn. Many wild roses can grow tall and straggly, usually in an effort to reach the light, and become quite ugly and a general nuisance. There is a simple but drastic remedy for this problem that rarely fails. In the late autumn or early winter, saw the whole plant down to about 12in(30cm) from the ground. This can also be done as soon as flowering has finished. The result is a proliferation of young wood. The first growth after this treatment may not yield flower, but this is a small price to pay for a dramatic improvement to both the plant and garden.

PRUNING A SHRUB ROSE

Most shrub roses flower once in a season and respond well to some form of restraint. Try to retain the young canes that have grown from the base and cut back the old flowering branches produced the previous summer to within about 1in(2.5cm) of the main stem. Immediately after the summer flush of flower, it is sometimes possible to remove entire old flowering shoots along with the main stems. This allows more light to penetrate into the tree and encourages the growth of young canes that will flower the following summer.

Not many gardens have the space to grow wild roses with such abandon. This plant has been cleverly restrained by supporting it on a frame, thereby lifting it off the ground without destroying its character.

This is a younger branch that must be preserved.

Do not attempt to prune these plants in the spring.

A good saw is essential for pruning wild roses. Wear your oldest clothes and be sure to put on thick gardening gloves.

Stones may lodge in the lower branches of old trees. Remove them to avoid damage to the saw.

1 A wild rose will take kindly to the occasional removal of one or two old branches. These are easy to identify, as they turn brown with age. This work is best done in early winter.

2 Occasionally, an unsightly scar is left where a branch has been cut out. You can paint this with grafting wax or a suitable dressing obtainable from good gardening shops. Do not be tempted to use a wood preservative. If the scar is torn, clean it up first with a sharp knife.

3 Cutting out old branches is an easy operation but take care that, having sawn off the branch, you pull it out of the tree without causing any damage. If you should accidentally damage the top branches of the bush, trim them with a pair of sharp secateurs to neaten them up.

Pruning a bush rose

Both hybrid tea and floribunda bush roses are recurrent-flowering, which means that every branch has the potential to produce bloom. However, once the stem has fulfilled its function, it must either be removed or at least cut back. Most plants naturally accumulate a tremendous amount of small spindly wood, old parts of the plant die back and strong shoots need controlling. In the summer, this process is called dead-heading, but in spring, the treatment is more severe and is described as pruning. For the plant to realize its full potential, it is vital to remove the non-productive branches every spring, otherwise they will impede the performance of the plant during the following flowering season. In bush roses, this means cutting out considerable quantities of old wood. Pruning also helps to keep plants healthy, as weak shoots are natural habitats for overwintering diseases, and a plant needs a strong base if it is to support good, strong shoots. Prune bush roses in the spring. In the autumn, it is a good idea to cut the plant back by about a third overall. Reducing the height helps the plant to avoid wind damage and loosening of the roots in winter gales - the cause of more fatalities than hard weather.

1 This plant has survived the winter. If it is a newly planted or replanted specimen, it may need firming into the ground before being pruned.

2 Remove some older branches completely, using a good pair of long-handled pruners. Never use your best secateurs to cut out dead wood.

Left: 'Iceberg', a fine free-flowering bush rose, can be conventionally pruned or trimmed as a shrub. Trim off small branches that could harbor disease. An exceptional rose that will grow anywhere.

Ideally, cut this type of wood back in the autumn.

This flowering wood developed in the autumn and has been killed by frost.

3 The most important function of pruning is to remove the old, spindly growth, which will only harbor disease if left on the plant and reduce the quality of flower.

Never cut back to thin wood, as it cannot produce strong growth.

Some of this top growth will have young green buds that must be removed. They are premature and probably frost-damaged.

Cut the branch on the slant. It will heal more easily and a slanted cut will not harbor moisture that encourages disease.

4 Having removed old and diseased branches, proceed to reduce the remaining wood by two thirds, the average proportion for most varieties.

5 Cut back the branch to an outside eye - a dormant bud growing outwards. Buds growing towards the center produce an unattractive bush.

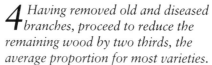

6 Resist the temptation to 'light' prune - bush roses are never damaged by hard pruning. Cut out all damaged branches.

7 As the pruning proceeds and the bush reveals itself, look it over to make sure you have not missed a dead branch.

8 The final result is a neat, clean-looking plant devoid of all rubbish. Leave a good framework of strong wood to produce a later harvest of bloom.

Pruning climbers and ramblers

Climbers and ramblers respond well to good pruning. During their first three formative seasons, climbers and ramblers require little maintenance other than heavy dead heading of the flowering shoots, but be sure to tie in the vigorous new shoots throughout the growing season. The season for serious pruning is in the late autumn, when the old wood is easier to identify. Securing branches to some form of support is vital. Varieties that produce very vigorous growth - usually ramblers - require maximum support and are better suited to pergolas and arches. Wire tautly secured on walls is ideal for less rampant varieties. Without any support at all, climbers and ramblers will grow into great mounds of flower. Leaving plants to grow in this form, however, will encourage disease and makes them extremely difficult to maintain.

Cut back the old shoots that produced flower last season, leaving a stump about 1in(2.5cm) long.

Cut out some of these very thin old shoots completely.

Never shorten these shoots until you have established the outline you wish to achieve.

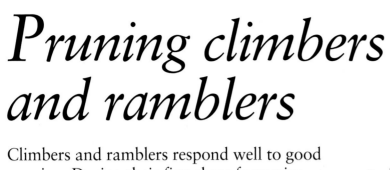

Right: *'Albertine' flowers briefly in midsummer. Tie in the ensuing growth so that it blooms the following year.*

1 First decide on the shape of the tree in relation to the area to be covered. Having established your plan of campaign, cut loose all the old strings holding the branches.

2 A rambler or summer-flowering climber produces long shoots that will bear flowers the following season. These are the branches that you must retain at all costs. Tie them in as they develop so that they are not damaged by the wind. Whatever form of support you choose, check it carefully every winter to make sure it is secure and able to sustain the weight of the plant. Remember that wooden poles can easily rot at ground level.

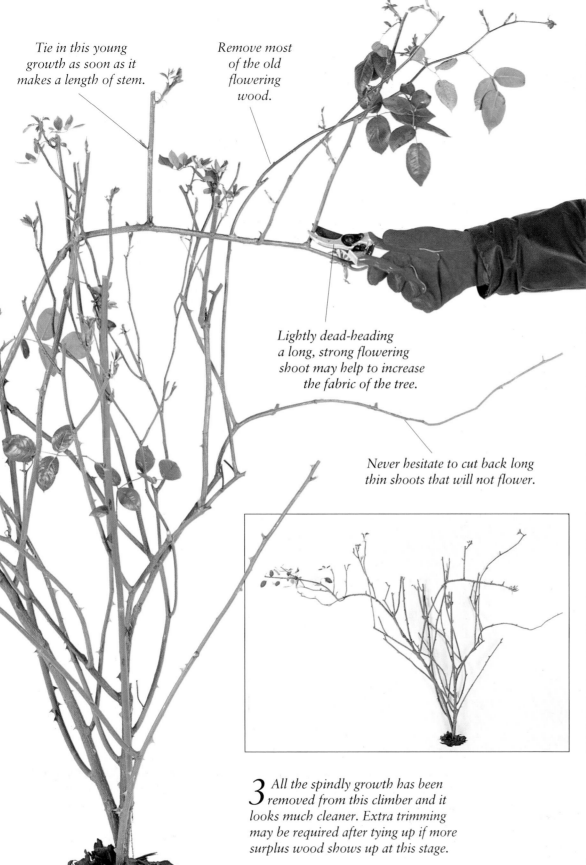

Tie in this young growth as soon as it makes a length of stem.

Remove most of the old flowering wood.

Lightly dead-heading a long, strong flowering shoot may help to increase the fabric of the tree.

Never hesitate to cut back long thin shoots that will not flower.

TYING A CLIMBING ROSE

The art of persuading a climbing plant to produce the maximum amount of flower is to create stress on the branches. This is done quite simply by bending them over in an arched fashion. A vertical stem will only flower at the end of the branch. The result of tying branches horizontally is that they not only produce more bloom, but will cover a greater area and new shoots are encouraged to grow from the base.

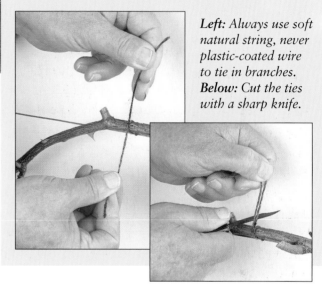

Left: *Always use soft natural string, never plastic-coated wire to tie in branches.* **Below:** *Cut the ties with a sharp knife.*

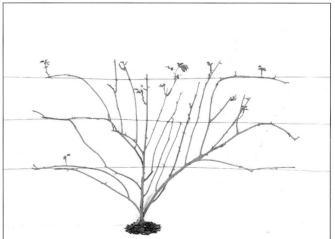

3 *All the spindly growth has been removed from this climber and it looks much cleaner. Extra trimming may be required after tying up if more surplus wood shows up at this stage.*

4 *A neatly secured plant will enhance the visual impact of the garden during the winter. The best time to carry out this work is in the late autumn, but not in frosty weather.*

49

Pruning a standard rose

A standard rose is a bush rose that has been propagated like any other rose but onto a stem that gives it height. Similarly, a shrub standard is a shrub on a stem and a weeper is a rambler on a tall stem. The same pruning principles apply to a standard variety as to the normal form, but bearing in mind the eventual shape of a standard in full flower, you may decide to keep a branch that you would have cut from a bush. Standards need a firm stake and the correct size strap to support them throughout the autumn and winter gales. Remove the strap regularly and test the strength of the stake; you may even find that the plant is supporting the stake! Replace the strap as the stem thickens up. Remember that the stem of a standard is some form of wild rose and may produce suckers. If you spot these early in the growing season, you can rub them off. Later in the year, you will need secateurs to remove them. If a standard is growing with bush roses, prune the bush roses first so you can reach the standard rose more easily.

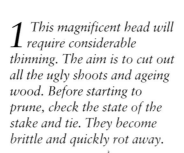

Right: 'Sweet Magic', a patio standard, grows to about 18in(45cm) high, with beautifully formed orange and gold fragrant blooms in perfect proportion to the healthy medium-green foliage.

1 This magnificent head will require considerable thinning. The aim is to cut out all the ugly shoots and ageing wood. Before starting to prune, check the state of the stake and tie. They become brittle and quickly rot away.

2 The first step is to thin out the plant, removing all the twiggy growth. This includes the occasional broken stem that is inevitable on such a wind-prone plant.

Occasionally you will have to take out an entire branch.

Always cut back the branch to within about 0.25in(6mm) above a bud.

3 When there is a good distribution of wood to prune, cut the plant back by about two thirds to three quarters compared to its original size. Achieving a well-shaped plant is more important than paying rigorous attention to the length of the stems.

The most common fault is leaving the central stems too long. Try and leave a flat top to the plant.

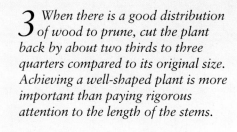

4 Cut the long central branches to achieve the desired flat top. Pruning standards is probably the most skillful operation in the rose garden - but involves no bending!

5 Already a good round shape is beginning to emerge, but examine the plant as you progress to see if more weak shoots have become apparent and be sure to cut these out.

Try to give shape to the basic structure of the plant, as well as to its final appearance. If some lower branches are broken or strained remove them completely.

6 The end result is a good distribution of sound wood, a neat flat top and the confidence that every branch will produce strong growth and many flowers.

Pruning a patio rose

Despite its relatively small size, the patio rose will require pruning in much the same way as its larger cousin, the bush rose. Many varieties rapidly accumulate twiggy wood, which can be an impediment to healthy and productive growth. Because the buds are so small, it is difficult to prune to an eye, so reduce the plant by about two thirds to three quarters and concentrate on cleaning up the plant. Patio roses amply repay a little extra attention at pruning time in early spring. As most of them are grown in the confines of a pot or in a small area of soil, refurbishing them will encourage a significant improvement in the results the following summer. As long as the plant is growing in the correct type of container, it may not be necessary to use a larger one when repotting. Repot the rose by knocking the plant out of its container and carefully checking the drainage. Remove about 2in(5cm) of soil at the base of the pot and replace it with a standard potting soil available from a garden shop. Then replace the plant and add a further 3in(7.5cm) of the new compost at the top. If the rose is growing in a restricted border, remove the top 3in(7.5cm) layer of soil and replace this with a good-quality soil. Complete your spring program by giving the plants a good-quality rose fertilizer. They need feeding like any other garden roses.

Below: 'Regensberg', a perfect small bush 12-18in(30-45cm) tall. An attractive patio rose that responds to correct pruning.

1 *Check the pot for frost damage and scrub it clean if necessary. Repot the rose before pruning it. Start by removing any broken branches.*

PRUNING A MINIATURE ROSE

Most miniature roses are grown from cuttings, which means that they grow on their own roots and must be cut back quite severely every spring. The prunings can be used to make new plants (see page 66). Pruning a miniature rose may seem to be an irksome task, but the results of cleaning up and cutting back quite hard are well worthwhile. Miniature roses grown in containers also benefit from annual repotting.

Left: Keep secateurs sharp for pruning. Miniatures appear to collect more rubbish at the base than most other roses. Clean the pot as well as tidying the plant.

For best results, trim the plant by about one third in autumn to reduce the risk of wind damage.

This wood can sometimes be used for cuttings in early spring.

Do not be afraid to cut off any growth that the plant has made during the winter. It has probably been damaged by frost.

Some of this growth is very soft and has been damaged by frost.

Quickly dispose of discarded wood.

Plants grow well in earthenware pots. Roots stay cooler and are less likely to dry out.

2 Patio roses may sustain quite a few broken branches. Once these have been eliminated, start to remove the twiggy growth and any dead material from the middle of the plant.

3 Remove the last of the long growths, as shown here. Check that you have not missed any dead wood.

A clean, well-pruned plant will give you pleasure throughout the growing season.

Make sure there is sufficient room in the pot to take water.

4 A perfectly repotted and well-pruned patio rose. A little bonemeal added to the top compost when repotting gives the rose a good start.

53

Rescuing a neglected plant

On average, you can expect to enjoy a well-tended garden rose for about 15 years, although this may be reduced to three or four years if a plant has been physically damaged, subjected to persistent disease or underfed. Some of these problems can be prevented and even remedied, given a program of good garden hygiene and maintenance. Many gardeners inherit potentially interesting plots containing sadly neglected plants and the first temptation is often to dig everything up, which is the worst thing to do. Allow a season to discover your garden, and in the meantime, remember that it is very hard to kill a rose plant by cutting it down. Neglected plants normally fade away because they are asked to support too much old wood and have not been properly fed. If you inherit a garden during the winter months, you can attack this problem in the early spring, which is the best time for dealing with old plants. However, it is often easier to identify a plant carrying a lot of dead wood during the early autumn months.

Right: 'Peace', with its soft yellow blooms edged with pale pink, is often found in a neglected garden. The large, medium-green leaves clothe an almost thornless plant. If a very early shoot should grow 'blind', cut it back to obtain a second crop of flower later on.

1 This is a typically tired plant, but it will soon respond to the correct pruning and care. Although secateurs are being used here, do not attempt to cut out tough, dead wood with your best pruners. A saw is a safer and more effective tool for this sort of task.

After removing a few old shoots, a neglected rose plant will revive rapidly.

2 Removing one or two old stumps can make a dramatic difference to the appearance of a neglected rose and makes the remaining fabric of the plant much easier to handle.

This excess of twiggy wood may be the result of greedy cutting for flower.

3 Some shoots only become evident after old stumps are eliminated. They are easily removed, but leave a clean cut that will not harbor disease.

This sort of wood harbors insects and fungus spores over winter. You can cut it out at any time.

4 The shoots at the base of the plant may have grown late in the season and were not sufficiently mature to withstand a hard winter. Examine the center of the stem, or pith, which should be a bright white. If it is brown, it means the stem is frosted and should be cut down hard.

Apply a deep mulch in early spring and feed regularly during the summer.

Once the stems have been reduced to this sort of height, they can be shortened by another 50 percent.

No bush has ever suffered by being cut down too much.

Wear a glove on your 'secateur' hand as protection from thorns on old wood.

5 Although much reduced, the fabric of the tree is still intact and with proper care will rapidly produce new growth as the season proceeds.

Below: Cut off the old rose head together with four leaves. Do not worry if this means removing buds, as these first few will only produce poor-quality bloom.

If time is short, simply snap off the head. Developing hips discourage new growth.

Seasonal maintenance

As we have seen, the rose is a very tolerant and adaptable plant, but it will certainly respond to regular attention during the growing season, particularly feeding. If well-rotted farmyard manure is available, apply it as a heavy mulch in late winter or early spring. Immediately after pruning, apply a basic rose fertilizer according to the manufacturer's instructions, followed by a second application immediately before the first flush of flower. Never apply a rose food after midsummer. You can control weeds with a rose bed weedkiller or by lightly hoeing the ground. Never dig the soil in an established rose bed, as this will damage and loosen the roots. If suckers appear from the wild rootstock, try to pull them out rather than cutting them off.

Apart from feeding, the best thing you can do for your plants is to dead-head them. Removing the old flowering heads not only prevents the development of hips, but also encourages the continuity of flower and a stronger second flush. There are many sprays on the market to control pests and diseases but, fortunately, modern roses are quite resistant to these afflictions. If you do buy a spray, follow the instructions on the container closely and wash all the spray equipment thoroughly after use. As the season progresses, climbers and ramblers will produce new growth. Make sure that you tie these growths in securely to avoid exposing the plant to wind damage. When the first frosts arrive, cut your rose bushes down by one-third to reduce rocking during the winter.

1 *All rose plants will benefit from a boost of fertilizer. Be sure to apply it before midsummer and take care not to let any fall on the base of the plant, as this could cause scorching.*

2 *Remember that hoeing the soil lightly not only removes weeds, but also improves the soil condition and helps to retain moisture. This is sometimes called a dust mulch.*

3 *You can also suppress weeds and retain moisture by using a mulch of peat or a peat substitute, such as pulverized bark. Apply when the soil is damp. There is little food in mulches.*

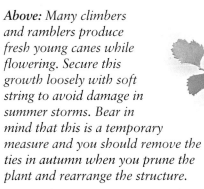

Above: Many climbers and ramblers produce fresh young canes while flowering. Secure this growth loosely with soft string to avoid damage in summer storms. Bear in mind that this is a temporary measure and you should remove the ties in autumn when you prune the plant and rearrange the structure.

1 Sometimes the stock on which the bush has been budded produces suckers. They are easy to recognize, as they grow from below ground level and have a 'wild' rose appearance.

2 If at all possible, try to remove the sucker by gently easing the ground and pulling the offending stem back to the main root system, where a good tug should solve the problem.

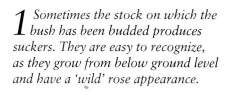

This is the complete sucker shown being pulled out of the ground in the above photographs. Fortunately, most modern roses are propagated on a rootstock that is sucker-free.

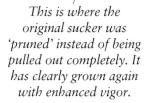

This is where the original sucker was 'pruned' instead of being pulled out completely. It has clearly grown again with enhanced vigor.

4 When spraying, make sure that your applicator can reach under the foliage. This is just as important as covering the top surface. Always follow the maker's instructions.

3 Traditionally, gardeners assumed that all growths with seven leaves were suckers from briar rootstocks. This can be misleading, since many modern varieties have seven leaflets.

Winter protection

Modern rose plants are hardy specimens that can withstand a considerable degree of frost. Some rose enthusiasts go to extraordinary lengths to protect their plants during the winter months, while others appear to make no effort at all and yet their plants are strong enough to survive. The secret lies in feeding your plants at the right time. Early in spring, apply good-quality, well-prepared compost to raise the fertility of the soil. To harden roses to make them strong enough to face the cold, apply extra potash in early summer. In areas that experience very windy weather, cut down rose bushes to 24in (60cm) after the first frosts. In this way, their top growth will not rock in the wind and make the plants loose in the soil. You could also try covering them if you wish. Because roses grow in such a range of locations with a variety of climates, it is impossible to lay down specific rules concerning their care during the winter. However, there are some good general guidelines. Observing the plant life in your area will help you to establish a workable program of winter care. Never handle plants in a frozen condition. Never feed roses after midsummer or give them an excess of nitrogen. Ensure that all plants are secure for the winter and do not prune them until the ground has totally thawed out.

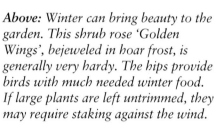

Hips can add color to your garden in winter.

Above: *Winter can bring beauty to the garden. This shrub rose 'Golden Wings', bejeweled in hoar frost, is generally very hardy. The hips provide birds with much needed winter food. If large plants are left untrimmed, they may require staking against the wind.*

Wrapping the head of a standard rose in straw protects it against the ravages of winter.

1 *In very hard conditions, you may need to cover the plant completely. Reduce the bush to about 12in(30cm).*

2 *Loosely fill a large container, such as an old garden pot, with straw and gently place it over the bush.*

3 *If you use old plastic buckets to cover plants, they will require stabilizing with a heavy weight.*

2 *In areas where frost damage can be expected, the commonest method of protection is to 'shroud' the entire plant. It is effective and cheap and the materials are easy to obtain.*

Place three or four canes around the plant to support garden netting or fine mesh chicken wire.

Do not use plastic, as it will hold moisture and cause the insulating material to break down and rot.

3 *Fill the enclosed space loosely with a dry material, such as shredded bark. This will help the rose to withstand the worst winter weather.*

Above: *In areas that experience hard winters and heavy frosts, the easiest way of protecting rose bushes is to earth up the base of the plants. If the top growth becomes damaged, then cut this down in spring and the plants will sprout as the temperature rises.*

Use a piece of netting that allows a generous height margin above the top of the plant.

4 *In the spring, remove the netting and prune the plant in the usual way after dispersing the insulating material around the bed as a mulch.*

Pests and diseases

To produce healthy plants, rose growers rely principally on a program of proper feeding and good hygiene. This means applying a good rose fertilizer at the appropriate time, but never a food that is high in nitrogen, unless you want big blooms for showing. Keep dead wood to a minimum and remove it in early autumn, when it is much easier to identify. The most common rose diseases are caused by fungi that find a haven in the plant. Sometimes they are simply unsightly, as in mildew, but black spot and rust cause leaf fall, which is harmful to plants. Spray affected roses with the appropriate product, carefully following the manufacturer's instructions. Pests are very easy to deal with; a good spray in early summer will discourage most of them. Identify the culprit, spray and systematically clean all utensils after use. In some places, rabbits and deer can become a nuisance. Although there are several remedies to discourage them, in the long term adequate fencing is the only solution. Occasionally, a rose is just not happy in a particular location. It becomes weak or appears never to thrive and is always the first to succumb to disease. If this happens, remove the plant rather than embark on expensive remedies. Unfortunately, there is nothing you can do to anticipate this problem.

Below: Black spot is a common and damaging fungus disease that will eventually result in the loss of infected leaves. Some varieties appear very prone to this disease and are being phased out.

Modern systemic sprays control the disease, but good husbandry and proper feeding are cheaper. Extra potash creates greater resistance.

Gather up and burn the diseased, fallen yellow leaves. Remove old and decaying wood that harbors dormant spores.

Left: Aphids, or greenfly, suck the sap on young rose shoots, but are easily controlled with modern systemic sprays or organically produced natural products.

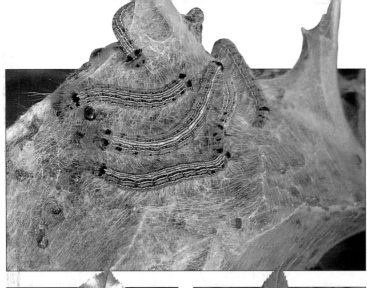

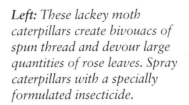

Left: *These lackey moth caterpillars create bivouacs of spun thread and devour large quantities of rose leaves. Spray caterpillars with a specially formulated insecticide.*

Right: *This white coating is caused by mildew, a fungal disease encouraged by high humidity. Some varieties are very prone to mildew; control it with regular spraying.*

Above: *Leaf-cutter bees, seasonal, short-lived predators, can cause this damage. Control by spraying.*

Above: *Unsightly galls, such as this spiked pea gall, are caused by wasps. Control these by using insecticides.*

Above: *Viruses have little effect on healthy roses. Good feeding is a help. Keep tools clean to avoid contamination.*

Below: *Cock chafers and Japanese beetles have a voracious appetite for roses. Simply pick them off by hand.*

Above: *Leaf-rolling sawflies produce this effect when they lay eggs in the leaves. Kill larvae by spraying soil in spring.*

Above: *Leaves infected with rust, a fungus, eventually turn yellow and drop off. Deter with a specialized fungicide.*

Propagating roses by budding - 1

You can increase your stock of roses in two main ways: by breeding a new variety by hybridization or by propagating the rose vegetatively. We look at how to breed a new rose on pages 68-71; in this section we consider how to perpetuate a particular rose variety by vegetative propagation. Just to confuse matters, you can propagate a rose either by budding it (sometimes mistakenly called grafting) or by taking cuttings. First we look at how to bud a rose.

Most modern roses are produced by budding the desired variety onto a vigorous rootstock, such as a wild briar or closely related species. This budding technique is carried out on millions of rose plants every year in nurseries around the world. With care, there is no reason why you cannot achieve success with budding your own roses. In a rose nursery, the briar rootstock will have been grown from a cutting or from seed. For your garden, you can obtain a briar from your local nursery and plant it during the spring. In midsummer, the briar should be big enough to take a bud. Having selected the rose variety you want to bud, follow the sequence shown here to isolate a single bud and prepare the briar rootstock to receive it.

2 *Trim the leaves from the stem straight away; delay might cause the stems to shrivel. The bark must be firm and the sap should still be active.*

Be sure to collect sticks of buds from healthy plants with no signs of disease or blemishes.

Cut the leaves back hard, leaving a short leaf stock which protects the bud inside.

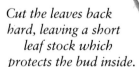

1 *Take good-quality budding wood from a stem that has recently flowered. Remove the flowering head together with the first three leaves.*

3 *If not required immediately, store this stick of buds in a cool moist atmosphere. Remove the thorns just before budding starts.*

PREPARING THE ROOTSTOCK

The briar planted in the spring will have developed by midsummer and be ready to receive the bud. Remove some soil to reveal the main stem of the stock, or collar, and clean away any extraneous dirt. Make a T-shaped cut and gently prise the bark open to reveal the paler sappy part inside. Do not cut too close to the top of the briar.

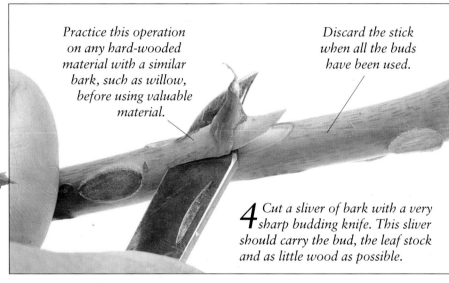

Practice this operation on any hard-wooded material with a similar bark, such as willow, before using valuable material.

Discard the stick when all the buds have been used.

4 *Cut a sliver of bark with a very sharp budding knife. This sliver should carry the bud, the leaf stock and as little wood as possible.*

The leaf stock is not an essential part of the operation, but does protect the bud and makes it easier to handle.

This big, fat bud has the potential to produce a first-class plant. If it appears black, discard it and start again.

5 *Reverse the sliver of bark and remove any wood that remains . It should come away easily. If not, it may be too dry and the bud will not 'take'.*

6 *Trim the base of the bark carrying the bud so that it looks neat and clean, and will slide snugly into the cut in the stock. This requires practice.*

7 *A perfectly prepared bud implant, ready for immediate insertion into the rootstock. The key to success is to work carefully but quickly.*

Propagating roses by budding - 2

Here we continue the budding sequence, beginning with the critical step of attaching the bud to the briar rootstock. Although the elasticity of the bark will hold the bud in place, securing the bark is the normal procedure. There are many ways of doing this, but using raffia is probably the easiest. Ensure that this is of good quality and pliable and that the bud is tied in quite tight. In a normal season, the raffia will naturally rot away, but sometimes you must remove it, but not before the following spring. Once this has been completed, simply leave the rootstock with its attached bud through the winter. On a frost-free day in late winter, cut the top off the briar to leave just a short neck above ground that bears the bud. (In nursery circles, this process is called 'heading back' or 'snagging'.) As the temperature increases during spring, the bud will begin to sprout, producing a fresh young branch about 6-9in(15-23cm) long by the middle of spring. If there are no late frosts, the branch will develop rapidly and the budded stock will form a rose bush in full flower by midsummer. That this new plant has arisen from the tiny bud attached to the rootstock during the previous growing season is a miracle of nature that fascinates even hardened nurserymen, year after year. When budding is carried out on a huge scale at a rose nursery, a 90 percent success rate of developing buds is considered very satisfactory. With care, your budded rose bush should mature during the summer months and be ready for you to lift in the autumn and plant out in its final position in the garden.

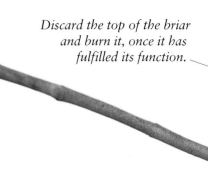

Discard the top of the briar and burn it, once it has fulfilled its function.

Use very sharp secateurs or long arms to cut back the stock about 0.3in(8mm) above the bud. The cut must be clean and not torn.

The bud has 'taken', forming a complete union with the stock. It usually remains dormant, but if it grows in early autumn, trim it back in the spring.

1 *Slide the prepared piece of bark carrying the bud into the cut made in the rootstock so that the implant fits neatly and the bud is uppermost.*

2 *You will need a length of pliable raffia about 15in(38cm) long. Working from the bottom upwards, carefully tie the bud to the rootstock.*

3 *Wind the raffia around the budded stock until it covers the cut, with the bud exposed. Tie off. Keep the area as clean as possible*

4 *During the winter months, leave the budded stock unprotected and the raffia will rot away. In early spring, cut the top off the rootstock.*

5 *As the sap starts to rise, the bud will begin to develop, slowly at first, but growth will be very rapid by early summer. By midsummer, a 'maiden' rose bush will produce its first fine blooms.*

This growth can accelerate very quickly, but you can encourage a quality plant by cutting the shoot back in mid-spring to produce a stronger plant.

Below: *This bloom of 'Keepsake' is typical of the quality that can be produced from a 'maiden' plant. Most rose displays at flower shows are cut from fields budded the previous year.*

As the young bud grows, there is considerable stress on the union of the stock and bud. It is at this time that a high wind can cause the buds to snap off.

Propagating roses by taking cuttings

The simplest way of propagating roses vegetatively is to take cuttings. It is easy to do, requires little knowledge of plant physiology and most gardeners have probably used this technique at some time or other with other plants. However, roses do pose a slight problem. Although they can all be grown from cuttings, the end results are not always as successful as you might expect, because the modern rose has apparently lost the ability to produce a satisfactory root system of its own. Recent research has shown that this trend can be reversed and it seems that the newest roses, particularly ground cover varieties, will grow just as well from cuttings as from budded plants. So which roses will grow from cuttings? Basically, most specie (wild) roses, old garden roses, many of the old ramblers and the majority of miniature and ground cover varieties will prosper as cuttings. Do not expect such good results from modern hybrid teas and floribundas, which are far more likely to produce top-quality blooms from budding (pages 62-65). However, growing your own plants is great fun and can give great satisfaction.

1 *Old ramblers are easy to grow from cuttings. Take a stem that has recently flowered, usually just after midsummer, and remove the old head.*

2 *Trim all but two of the remaining leaves, slightly gouging out the buds to encourage roots to grow. Use a sharp knife. Collect propagating material from healthy stock.*

Prepare a piece of stem about 9in(23cm) long, with the lower cut trimmed just below a bud.

3 *Produce a 'heal' by trimming the bottom leaf where the leaf joins the stem. Trim away a small amount of bud tissue and this will cause roots to develop at this point.*

4 *You can dip the finished cutting in a solution to encourage root growth, but this is not essential. Whether you use rooting powder or liquid, read all the instructions carefully. Never allow the cutting to dry out.*

5 *Prepare a trench to take the cuttings. It is a good idea to add some sharp sand in which to place the bases of the stems.*

6 *Place the cuttings in the trench so that each has about 1in (2.5cm) of stem with two leaves above ground level.*

7 *The most common cause of failure with rose cuttings is dehydration, which happens if too much of the cutting protrudes above the soil. Providing the cuttings with semi-shade for the first few months also helps to avoid this problem.*

The original leaves will fall off naturally, as the root system becomes established. Given a good growing season, you can plant the cuttings out in their permanent position about a year later.

Breeding a new rose - hybridization

Almost every modern rose is the product of hybridization - the cross-fertilization of one rose with another. This is a fairly simple process, as long as you understand the parts of a rose flower, observe meticulous attention to hygiene in the hybridizing unit - usually a greenhouse - and keep good records. Like most flowers, the rose is bisexual, with male stamens bearing pollen surrounding the female stigma that receives pollen during fertilization. During controlled pollination from a selected male donor, the flower destined to be the female partner must be deprived of its own pollen to prevent self-fertilization. In most temperate climates, the summer season is not long enough to ripen the hips outdoors after fertilization. Growing the parent plants in a greenhouse, although not necessarily with heat, is the best strategy. As they will be under glass for about 10 months, choose containers of about 5 gallons (23 liters) capacity. Select the prospective parents and pot them on in early autumn. A well-established two- or three-year-old potted plant will give a greater number of flowers and hips. Bring them into the greenhouse in midwinter, keeping them well watered but not overfed. Even without heat they will flower in late spring. Hybridization can begin now and should be completed by early summer. After this, water sparingly and remove any extraneous growth. By late autumn, the hips will be ripe and ready to harvest.

Right: *To pollinate a flower you must have access to the essential parts of the plant when the petals are well formed. Removing petals too early will damage the plant, too late and the pollen will ripen and be released.*

1 Remove the petals cleanly, by holding the calyx - the bottom part of the flower - with one hand and removing the petals with the other.

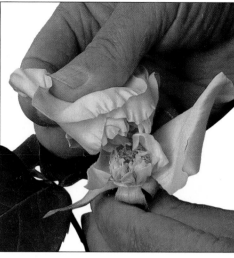

2 When you have removed the petals, you will be able to see the stamens. These are the male, pollen-bearing parts of the flower.

Remove the stamens and keep them in a dry dish for later use. The pollen is viable for about three weeks.

3 The most painstaking part of the operation is removing the stamens to create an all-female head. You must complete this before the pollen is ripe.

4 *After removing the petals and stamens, wait for 24 hours. This allows time for the female stigma to become receptive to fertilization.*

You can tell when the stigma is receptive to fertilization because it appears sticky.

Use a fine camel hair brush to transfer the pollen. Sterilize it before using it for the next plant.

Once you have used a flower, remove it completely to avoid a build-up of decaying vegetation in the area.

Do not remove any other part of the flower.

5 *This is the delicate operation of fertilization. Gently brush the pollen onto the ripe stigma. One application is more than enough.*

6 *Once the operation is complete, allow the fertilized flower to develop in a dry atmosphere; it should ripen in about four to five months.*

Label each fertilized hip with the name or number of the male parent and the date. Record details in the seedling (stud) book.

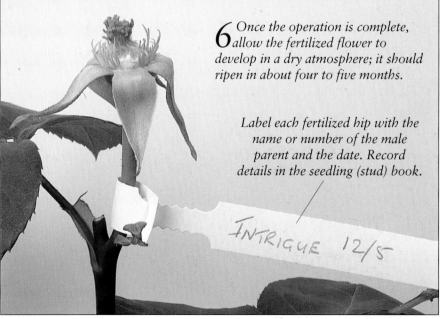

INTRIGUE 12/5

Breeding a new rose - raising seed

Breeding a new rose is not complete until hips are harvested and the seed sown and successfully germinated into new plants. However, there may be problems along the way. The parents may not compatible, for example, or one may be sterile. Simply removing the petals and stamens may damage the flowerhead so that the young hips appear to rot. If everything goes to plan, remove the hips in late autumn and store them in a cool, damp medium, such as damp peat or vermiculite for about three months. This enforced dormancy - called stratification - is necessary to induce the rose seeds to germinate. A short period of freezing also encourages germination. Take the hips out of the medium in late winter, extract the seeds and sow them in a mix of sand and soil. Germination can take from two to eight weeks. The young seedlings grow quite slowly but can be spurred on with a little heat. Most seedlings will produce flower by midsummer, but will only give an indication of color. For a real assessment of the new hybrid's potential you will need to bud them on (see pages 62-65) immediately after the flower has faded. Alternatively, plant the seedlings out in the autumn so that they flower during the following summer.

1 In order to raise healthy seedlings, use top-quality, sterilized seed compost. Sow the seeds in pots or in a deep seed tray and firm the soil in thoroughly.

Always use clean seed trays and pots; good hygiene is essential.

Right: *Extracting seed is a laborious task. Some hips will only contain one seed, others a great many. Do not be surprised to find the occasional empty pod.*

The label identifies the parent plants.

Seeds vary in size. Sow them straight away.

2 Sow the seeds in an orderly way, leaving about 1in(2.5cm) of space between them. Label them accurately so that you can check the germination rate as the seedlings appear.

Rose seed is not easy to germinate and you will need great patience. Protect the seeds from mice!

4 Germination can be erratic. Seedlings of this size will take six to eight weeks to grow and will produce flower after a further three weeks.

Below: The lovely 'Sheila's Perfume' was bred by an amateur hybridist and has won many awards for fragrance and as a good garden rose.

Use good-quality, coarse sand. Make sure it is lime-free and well sterilized.

A seed tray with ample drainage is essential. The greater the depth of soil, the better the quality of the seedlings produced.

3 Finally, cover the seedlings with a layer of coarse sand about 0.5in (1.25cm) thick. Rose seed takes a long time to germinate and this surface discourages the development of lichen.

Showing roses

Showing the fruits of your success in the garden can be a source of great pride. Indeed, many flower societies were first established so that members could compete to produce and show the biggest and best blooms. A well-grown rose is one of the easiest flowers to prepare and exhibit on the show bench. When selecting show blooms, remember that healthy foliage can contribute just as much to a successful exhibit as a superb flower. In order to enhance the size of the bloom, it is a good idea to give your roses an extra application of a nitrogenous feed - dried blood is best - in late spring. Before cutting any blooms for a show, fill some large containers with water and add a compound that encourages the cut flower to take up water. You can buy this preparation from a garden center or florist. A common mistake that exhibitors make is to leave everything to the last minute. Try to cut hybrid tea roses showing seven or eight petals about two days before exhibiting them. Plunge them into the prepared water and stand them in semi-darkness. They will grow in size but will not develop. When transporting roses to a show, pack them tightly with other blooms or wrap them in newspaper; never use tissue paper as it sticks to the blooms. On arrival at the show, give the blooms some time to develop and warm up. Cold petals are brittle and easily bruised when dressed for showing. (Dressing rose petals involves manipulating them gently with your fingers to create a fuller shape.) There are several methods of staging your roses, so refer to the show schedule for guidance. Finally, allow time to label your blooms clearly, which is bound to impress the judges.

1 *Most hybrid tea bush roses will develop side shoots. Remove these to allow the center bloom to grow bigger. This is called disbudding.*

2 *It is important to remove these lateral growths as soon as they appear. Take great care not to tear the stem or damage the leaves.*

Right: *The judges will deduct points for split blooms, as here. Dirty flowers will also lose points. Check your roses carefully before displaying them.*

Below: *Cut your potential prize winners late in the evening or early in the morning. Remove the lower leaves and place the stems in deep prepared water in a cool place. Allow plenty of time for the blooms to develop.*

1 You can wrap each stem in newspaper for transportation. If necessary, tie the developing bloom with thick strands of soft wool to prevent damage to the outside guard petals. Remove ties before judging.

2 Once wrapped, pack the blooms tightly in buckets filled with the same water that was prepared for cutting. A broad-based, tall bucket, as shown here, is very stable and particularly suitable for floribundas.

3 If half-opened blooms need a little encouragement to open out, coax them with a soft brush or manipulate them gently with your fingers.

'Elina' ('Peaudouce') is almost unbeatable if grown to perfection.

'Just Joey' can produce huge blooms.

'Loving Memory' is a classic show bloom with a perfectly formed, high center.

A clean example of the pale 'Polar Star' always attracts the judges.

Cut 'Peace' young for showing.

'Keepsake's' high-pointed center makes it ideal for showing.

'Ingrid Bergman', a prolific, dark red rose, needs careful disbudding.

4 A typical example of a class for seven specimen HT blooms. Arrange them with care to achieve a balance of color and height.

Part Two

DISPLAYING ROSES

The rose has always been one of the most important flowers to be used as a decoration and we can trace its history from the petal-strewn floors of Roman palaces, through medieval church garlands of red and white roses to our more conventional uses of this special flower today. It has always held great symbolism and meaning throughout the world, sometimes acting as a religious token or the emblem of a country, often conveying a lover's message and constantly inspiring poets and artists to new heights of creativity.

Roses have been grown commercially as cut flowers for many years and their large color range and strong stems have made them justifiably popular. However, the home-grown rose has several advantages over its shop-bought cousin and one of the most significant of these is its fragrance, which has been lost in many varieties sold as cut flowers. The fragrance of roses is important for bouquets, posies and flower arrangements in the home, and people always expect a rose to smell delicious and are disappointed when it does not. The variety of shape, formation, texture and color of garden roses is also vast, compared with the relatively few varieties on offer at the florist.

It may seem impossible to choose the best types for picking, but first decide how you are going to use your cut roses and then make your choice according to this and the garden space you have to grow them. Long-stemmed flowers are desirable for many arrangements, but you can create just as many beautiful decorations using short-stemmed roses, floribundas, sprays of climbing and rambling varieties, even miniature and old-fashioned types. This section of the book shows you how.

An informal arrangement of pink roses, spray carnations and eucalyptus.

Preparing your roses

There are very few preparation techniques that apply only to roses except, perhaps, removing the vicious thorns from the stems of certain varieties. There are a few preparatory stages to go through before you begin to arrange roses for indoor displays, but most are very practical and a matter of common sense. If you can, pick roses early in the day when it is cool or in the evening, as this is when the plant is transpiring least. A rose picked in the middle of a hot summer day will rapidly wilt. All cut flowers benefit from a conditioning period, which simply means leaving them to stand in cool water for several hours before using them in a display. It is well worth doing this with all flowers to make sure that they live as long as possible once cut from the growing plant.

Below: Using sharp scissors, secateurs or a special tool, clip away any sharp thorns. Some florists run up the stem with a blade, but this takes practice.

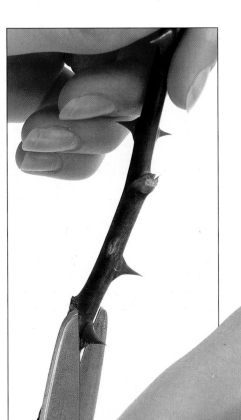

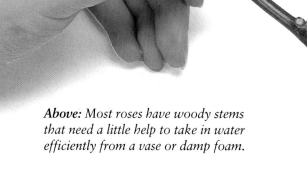

Above: Most roses have woody stems that need a little help to take in water efficiently from a vase or damp foam.

Above: Always cut a rose stem at a sharp angle, leaving as large a surface area as possible touching the water. Ideally, you should recut the stem each time you take it out of water for a while, to expose fresh tissue again.

Rather than just slice across the stem, cut a slit a little way up the stem to reveal a larger surface area.

Below: *Another method of increasing the surface area is to crush the lower part of the stem with a hammer or mallet. Make sure you do this on a wooden board or other solid surface.*

Splitting the stem may make arranging the roses in florist foam a bit more difficult.

Use a hammer or another heavy object, such as a rolling pin, for crushing stems.

A mixture of long-stemmed hybrid tea roses picked from the garden.

Above: *When all the stems have been cut and prepared, stand the roses in a deep container with a small amount of cool (but not icy) water and leave them to drink for several hours or overnight. This will prolong the life of the roses, once arranged.*

Basic floristry techniques

Once your flowers are conditioned and ready to use, there is little more to be done. For a few special decorations, such as posies, bridal bouquets and circlets, it is useful to know how to wire a rose. This involves creating a thin and flexible replacement stem that you can move into any position. Also, a bunch of wire stems in a posy takes up less space than the same number of thick stems. Occasionally, a bunch of roses will wilt dramatically. The method described on these pages for saving them does not always work, but will usually bring them round. Wilting can be caused by stems drying out and then being unable to take up water properly, so always keep cut stems of unused roses under water, even while you are working and arranging. Finally, garden roses dry beautifully and very easily and it is well worth picking a few through the summer for this purpose. Dry them one at a time or several together and by the end of the summer you should have a beautiful collection for winter decorations.

Stopping the wilt

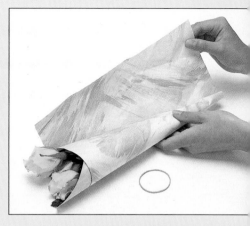

1 *Recut all the stems at an angle and stand them immediately in a small amount of boiling water for about 2 minutes.*

2 *Roll the bunch of roses tightly in some stiff paper and secure the wrapping with a rubber band. This also protects the roses during handling.*

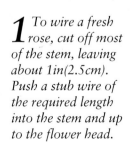

Ready-cut stub wire for flower arranging is available in different lengths and thicknesses and usually sold by weight.

1 *To wire a fresh rose, cut off most of the stem, leaving about 1in(2.5cm). Push a stub wire of the required length into the stem and up to the flower head.*

Stem, or gutta, tape is available in green, brown and white. Green is the most useful for fresh bouquets and posies.

2 *Starting just under the rose head, take a piece of stem tape and twist and wrap it round the stem and down over the wire, too. It sticks to itself under pressure from your fingers.*

3 Stand the flowers in their wrapping in a container of cool water for several hours or until the roses have revived and look fresh.

Home-dried roses

Drying roses at home is simple and made even simpler if you have a constant source of warmth over which you can hang the drying flowers. A solid fuel cooker or kitchen range is ideal, but a boiler, airing rack or even a greenhouse will do. The aim is to dry the flowers quickly to preserve their color. They shrink quite a lot, but also open out a little after they have been hanging up. Either hang up roses complete with stems (as shown here) or cut fresh rose heads, leaving a small piece of stem and attach a wire to them (see page 78). Hang them above the heat source, either singly or in a bunch. The wire will rust and bed tightly into the rose. As soon as the roses are thoroughly dried, remove them and store in a dry dark place.

These roses have been left to dry on their own stems.

A fine bunch of fresh roses hanging up to dry.

The same roses, ready to use in an arrangement after drying.

Fairly full hybrid tea, floribunda or old-fashioned roses are the best for drying.

Scarlet red and yellow roses are two of the best colors for drying.

A selection of roses

1 Hybrid tea 'Ingrid Bergman'.

2 Hybrid tea bush rose 'Troika'.

3 Floribunda bush rose 'Picasso'.

4 *Rosa rugosa* 'F. J. Grootendorst'.

5 Hybrid tea bush rose 'Polar Star'.

6 *Rosa rugosa alba*.

7 Modern shrub rose 'Graham Thomas'.

8 Floribunda bush rose 'Intrigue'.

9 Ground cover rose 'Nozomi'.

10 Old garden rose *R. alba* 'Félicité Parmentier'.

11 Old garden rose *R. centifolia muscosa* 'White Bath'.

12 Hybrid tea bush rose 'Royal Highness'.

13 Hybrid tea bush rose 'Blessings'.

14 Old garden rose *R. gallica* 'Charles de Mills'.

15 Old garden rose *R. centifolia* 'Petite de Hollande'.

16 Climbing rose 'Gloire de Dijon'.

17 Old garden rose *R. bourboniana* 'Honorine de Brabant'.

The range and choice of garden roses is vast and bewildering, but this selection features some typical examples from many of the rose types and families, ranging from old garden roses to modern hybrid teas and floribundas, all of which are suitable for flower arranging and display.

18 Hybrid tea bush rose 'Grandpa Dickson'.

19 Wild rose specie *Rosa webbiana*.

20 Hybrid tea bush rose 'Heart Throb' ('Paul Shirville').

21 Wild rose specie *Rosa eglanteria* (Sweetbriar). Scented foliage.

22 Hybrid tea bush rose 'King's Ransom'.

23 Floribunda bush rose 'Chinatown'.

24 Old garden rose hybrid perpetual 'Souvenir de Dr. Jamain'.

25 Old garden rose *Rosa gallica* 'Officinalis' (Apothecary's rose).

26 Hybrid tea bush rose 'Fragrant Charm 84' ('Royal William').

27 Old garden rose *R. alba* 'Königin von Dänemark' ('Queen of Denmark').

28 Rambler rose 'Francis E. Lester'.

29 Rambler rose 'Seagull'. Highly scented.

30 Miniature rose *R. rouletii*.

31 Floribunda bush rose 'The Queen Elizabeth Rose'.

32 Old garden rose *R. alba* 'Celeste' ('Celestial').

The classic choice

The rose has many moods and can be used in hundreds of different ways as a floral decoration. If asked to describe an arrangement of roses, many people would probably recall the traditional ways in which they have seen it displayed, such as the one immaculate bloom in a tall narrow vase or an old-fashioned silver rose bowl filled with nothing but exquisitely perfect flowers. These days, few of us live in very formal surroundings and have little need for this kind of arrangement, but there are times when a classic approach is appropriate for a special occasion or simply to add a traditional look to a room. The rose is a classic amongst flowers and sometimes it deserves to be displayed in a way that enables it to live up to its great reputation. The next few pages should inspire you with new ideas on a formal theme.

Using a classic porcelain vase

A classic flower-decorated porcelain vase needs a careful choice of flowers to fill it. Here, the painted flowers on the china provide the cue for what to put in it and the best colors to choose. Roses are the important feature, but they have been mixed with complementary garden flowers and foliage that form a framework and pleasing background to the blooms. This vase is designed to be seen from the front and therefore the arrangement faces forwards and is ideal to put on a side table, shelf or any piece of furniture that stands against a wall. The mix of colors may seem unconventional, but apart from one strong red accent, most are soft pastels. The final effect of the whole arrangement is harmonious and very pretty.

2 *Make an initial choice of flowers and bunch them to see how the colors work together. This will help you to estimate how much material you will need.*

Recut flower stems, then split any woody ones and trim away the lower foliage.

1 *Tape a block of damp floral foam securely into the vase leaving it well proud of the vase rim. Add more water as a reservoir to sustain the flowers once they have been inserted.*

In this arrangement, keep the amount of foliage to a minimum to leave space for plenty of different flower varieties.

Replace shorter-lived flowers as they fade to give the arrangement a longer life.

5 Complete the arrangement with filler material, such as Alchemilla mollis *and small-flowered, scented white 'Seagull' roses. Let a few flowers curve naturally down to the table.*

3 *Arrange tall stems in a fan shape across the back of the vase to create an outline and add a trailing stem at one side.*

The roses are old-fashioned and modern types. The multi-petaled old roses have the right feel for this traditional look.

4 *Continue filling in the display with shorter stems of phlox, alstroemeria and roses. Position them so that they are evenly spaced throughout and near to the front.*

Remember to top up the water level frequently, as there is a great deal of plant material in a small container.

1 *Begin by carefully cutting off any thorns and leaves that are likely to be under water in the vase. Leave any good foliage just below the flower head. Recut the base of the stem at a long slant.*

Pink roses in an elegant glass vase

3 *Start to arrange the rose stems one at a time in the vase, working round and spacing them evenly.*

Some vases are classic in their shape. This curvy glass one makes any flower displayed in it look elegant and timeless. However, the narrow neck means that only a few stems can fit in it, so choose roses with large flower heads for the maximum effect. A glass container will obviously show the stems inside, so be sure to strip off any small leaves and thorns leaving clean, neat stalks on view. Change the water daily too, so that it is kept clear and sparkling. Stand the finished arrangement in a light position and lower than standing eye-level, so that the perfect blooms are seen to best advantage. You could choose any color rose for this type of arrangement, from strong scarlet to soft peach, but it will have the most impact with just a single color. Here, the rose type is an exquisite pale pink hybrid tea.

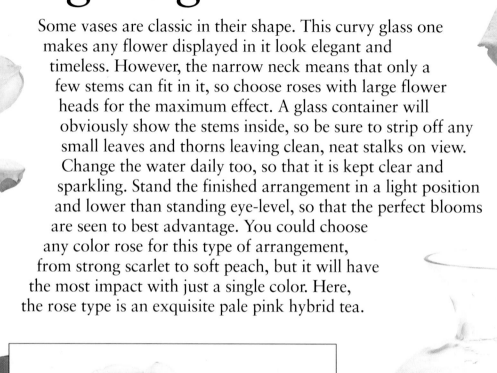

2 *Pull away any odd, stained, damaged or ugly outside petals to make a perfect bloom. Never take off more than one or two petals, otherwise the flower will look thin.*

Make the arrangement an all-round one to be viewed from any angle.

4 Add more blooms to create a cluster of flower heads in a curving shape that reflects the curves of the base below. Loosen the heads so that they are not crushed and have a little air and space around them.

If the stems are slightly short for the vase, fill the base with clear glass marbles.

Red roses, carnations and eucalyptus

1 Trim off lower stems and leaves from each spray of eucalyptus and cut all stems to the same length. Begin to put them into the vase, working round in a circle.

2 With the eucalyptus in place, add carnations throughout the foliage, working evenly all over the arrangement. Use some shorter stems at the outer edges.

3 Finally add the roses, spacing them out equally throughout the arrangement between the carnations. Aim to create a smooth continuous outline above the vase.

The blue-green eucalyptus leaves make a perfect foil for the strong crimson-red spray carnations and long-stemmed roses.

Bridesmaid's rose and ivy circlet

A small circlet of fresh flowers for a bridesmaid is not as difficult to make as it might appear. Once you have mastered how to wire each flower head and leaf, the rest is simple. Although the circlet will stay fresh for several hours, it is a good idea to make it as near to the event as possible. When complete, you can spray it with a fine mist of water to help it remain fresh, and then keep it covered under a single sheet of damp tissue paper until it is needed. The first thing to do is to measure the child's head accurately and to make the basic circlet, either with florist's wire or milliner's fabric-covered wire. Add a little extra to the circumference to allow for the thickness of the wires that attach the flowers to the circlet. Any small roses or rose buds are suitable, including miniature varieties.

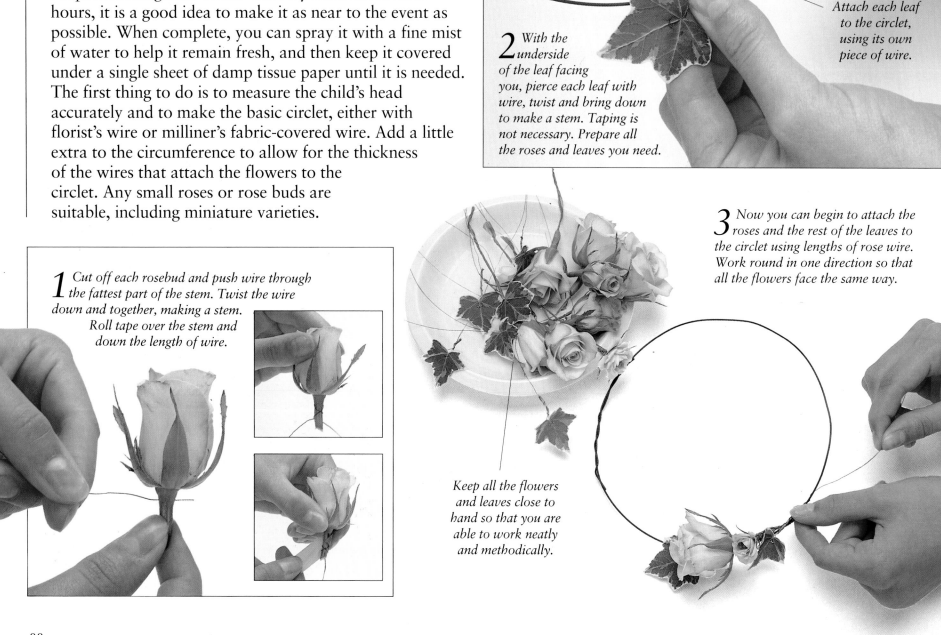

2 *With the underside of the leaf facing you, pierce each leaf with wire, twist and bring down to make a stem. Taping is not necessary. Prepare all the roses and leaves you need.*

Attach each leaf to the circlet, using its own piece of wire.

3 *Now you can begin to attach the roses and the rest of the leaves to the circlet using lengths of rose wire. Work round in one direction so that all the flowers face the same way.*

1 *Cut off each rosebud and push wire through the fattest part of the stem. Twist the wire down and together, making a stem. Roll tape over the stem and down the length of wire.*

Keep all the flowers and leaves close to hand so that you are able to work neatly and methodically.

If necessary, you can add more ivy leaves to fill in any large gaps or spaces in the final circlet.

A small-leaved variegated ivy makes the perfect foliage, as it is light and delicate but provides enough color contrast.

Ideal plants to use in a circlet

The fundamental construction of a circlet remains the same whatever plants you choose to use. For an older bridesmaid or a bride, you might want to use larger, more lavish roses to create a fuller and more stunning effect. Always choose foliage that is quite tough, such as ivy, leather fern, myrtle or something similar and that will not wilt too soon. Roses are always an excellent choice for a circlet, as they can be pinned through their calyx to keep them tightly in bud. Spray carnations, lily of the valley, stephanotis, ranunculus, lilies and orchids are just some of the other suitable flowers for this treatment. You could also consider many garden flowers, leaves and berries, which all make a lovely and informal addition to home-made bridal decorations.

4 Continue wiring the roses and ivy right around the circlet, alternating single larger roses with two or more miniature roses. Be sure to cover the circlet completely.

You could try adapting this scheme for making a circlet to decorate a hat. For added variety, choose larger and quite different roses.

89

Pure white spray carnations are a perfect posy flower. They last well and are solid and neatly shaped.

Victorian rosebud posy in red, white and pink

Small, hand-held posies, or tussie-mussies as they were once called, have been popular for centuries. Ideally, they should contain strongly scented flowers to give the most pleasure. This small posy is made in organized rings of different colors and types of flowers, based on the kind of posy a Victorian girl might have carried. A version of this idea is perfect for a small bridesmaid to carry at a wedding and there is no reason why a larger posy made with more rings of flowers should not make a beautiful bridal bouquet. The design looks complicated, but is very easy to make, as it falls naturally into place if the flowers in each ring are the same size. A rose or rosebud is the classic central flower, no matter what flowers make up the remainder of the posy. The last ring of a posy is often made from an edging of fern leaves or other foliage or even a paper frill to finish it off neatly. Here the fluffy flower heads of love-in-a-mist make an unusual and attractive edging.

1 *Choose one beautiful rose bloom as the center starting point and hold it in one hand. Then begin to build up a ring of carnations around it, using the other hand.*

Wiring at this point in the process means that you can relax and let go of the bunch if you need to.

You can use rubber bands, florist wire or string to tie the bunch of flowers together.

2 *Complete the white circle and then start a circle of alternate pink roses and paler carnations outside it, holding it steady in one hand all the time. Tie it firmly after this stage.*

Trim off the stems to the same length, using secateurs or a pair of sharp scissors.

Spray carnations or garden pinks have a sweet, spicy smell that blends well with the scent of roses.

4 *The finished posy should be comfortable to hold, so do not be tempted to make it over large by bunching too many stems together.*

3 Complete the posy with a final ring of love-in-a-mist or other appropriate flowers or foliage around the edge. Tie the whole bunch once again, winding wire tightly round the stems just below the flower heads.

Finish off the whole posy with a toning ribbon tied into a bow. This posy is decorated with wire-edged ribbon that is simple yet elegant.

Lapel decorations for that special occasion

There are still certain formal occasions when people are expected to wear a lapel decoration and other less formal events where it simply adds style and a touch of fun. There is no need to order an expensive one from the flower shop as it is a very simple piece of floristry to put together yourself, using home-grown flowers, as long as you chose varieties that will not wilt too quickly. A garden rose makes an imaginative and scented decoration compared with the dull and ubiquitous carnation. If you make it larger than a one- or two-flower version, you have a fine corsage suitable for a dressy suit, a ballgown or even a wedding hat.

3 Take another flower, (here it is a freesia), and put it against the rose but extending slightly beyond it. Cut both the stems to the same length.

Choose flowers that will stand this treatment, such as roses and freesias.

If you prefer, you could use different foliage, such as fern or a perfect rose leaf.

1 Choose a well-shaped, tightly closed bud and cut it off the main stem, leaving about 2in (5cm) of stem below the bud.

1 Choose a perfect bloom that is just at the point of opening from the bud stage and cut it away from the main stem, trimming away foliage and thorns.

2 Select a short trail of variegated ivy and cut away the lower leaves, leaving the stem clear. The ivy should be slightly longer than the rose stem to show behind the bloom.

4 Arrange the three stems of rose, freesia and ivy in your hand, with the rose at the front. If possible, hold the flowers against the clothes that are to be worn.

5 Bind the stems closely withgreen tape, working from the flower heads down the stems. Cover the cut stem ends and bring the tape back up, squeezing it tightly before cutting it.

Setting off with a fern

2 Snip off a piece of leather fern to put behind the bud. The fern should be a little longer than the bud.

3 Wrap tape tightly around both stems, twisting and squeezing as you work down. Wind the tape back up the stem a little way and then cut off.

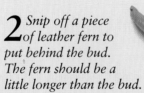

6 Attach with an extra-long, fine dressmaker's pin from behind the fabric or put through a buttonhole and pin securely under the lapel.

Easy and informal

Roses not only look wonderful on their own, but they are also one of the best flowers to mix with other varieties. They are good natured and easy to deal with when it comes to making all kinds of arrangements. These days, many people love to have flowers in the house but do not want to spend hours putting them together. Fashions, too, have changed and relaxed and informal arrangements that fit in with our interiors and our lifestyle are the order of the day. Flowers that look simple and unfussy without lots of complicated mechanics are what most of us want, except perhaps for special occasions. Roses have a substance and a style of their own so that just a couple of blooms in a china mug will look bright and decorative, even though the arrangement takes just five minutes to put together.

Pink Felicia roses in a moss-lined wire basket

Rose arrangements do not always have to be created on a grand scale or even be particularly large. Many varieties of garden rose lend themselves perfectly to simple, small decorations of the kind you might stand amongst a collection of favorite objects on a shelf or occasional table or in a guest bedroom. These simple, informal ideas are quick to produce and can make such a difference to any room. Both the ideas on these pages use scented roses and flowers, and both are displayed in unusual containers. Be open to new ideas when you come to select a vase and begin looking in the kitchen or china cupboard for old-fashioned bowls or molds or any suitable cookware that might make unusual flower containers. Small wire-mesh baskets are very popular for displaying all kinds of things and, when lined with moss, they are especially pretty for rose arrangements.

1 Push a block of foam into the container and mark where to cut it. Leave it slightly proud of the rim to allow more height for arranging.

1 Soak some sphagnum moss until it is completely wet and then squeeze it until just damp. Line the basket on the base and all round the sides.

Use suitable moss from the garden, or buy it from a florist or garden center.

The moss is just a disguise for the foam that goes inside the basket.

2 Use a small cylinder of florist foam or cut a piece to fit snugly inside the basket. Make the foam wet and push it firmly into place inside the moss lining.

You could line the base with plastic or stand the finished arrangement on a mat to protect the surface beneath.

Roses in a jelly mold

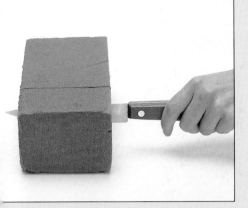

2 Remove the foam and slice it cleanly through with a sharp kitchen knife. Then wet the foam and push it tightly back into the container.

3 Begin to fill in the foam with stems of honeysuckle. Spread them all over the arrangement, spacing them out as equally as possible.

4 For extra variety, you can add a few different flowers, such as apricot digitalis and yellowy cream alstroemeria.

These are blooms from the delicately colored floribunda rose, 'Cafe'.

3 Fill the basket with small pieces of a floribunda or old-fashioned rose with buds and open flowers on the same stem.

4 Fill the basket generously so you have a full, rounded outline of roses. Mist it with a fine spray at regular intervals to keep both the moss and roses fresh.

The subtle pale pink hybrid musk rose 'Felicia' is generous with both blooms and scent.

Old-fashioned country roses in rustic baskets

Every kind of basket, whether it is smooth and shiny or rough and twiggy, has an affinity with roses. They complement each other very well and the rustic texture of willow, hazel or cane sets off the rich colors and velvety petals of garden roses to perfection. Old-fashioned, scented roses with wonderful, full-petaled heads in dense shades of raspberry, crimson and deep, glowing pinks are especially suitable for filling country-style baskets. The popular rambler 'Albertine', for example, with its lax stems and drooping heads, looks entirely at home in a twig basket. Both the versions of basket arrangements shown on these pages make use of roses in quantity alone, which produces a very strong look and undiluted texture and color. However, if you prefer, you could mix the roses with other flowers and plant material for a slightly different effect. If you do choose to do this, be sure to use at least a proportion of three-quarters roses to one-quarter other material.

1 *Metal foil is excellent for lining a deep basket as it easier to mold up the sides than plastic. It will provide a durable and waterproof 'container' within the basket. However, take care not to tear it as you put it in place.*

An 'Albertine' basket

Below: *Plunge a complete block of floral foam under water and hold it there until it no longer bobs above the surface or as specified by the maker.*

Left: *Make the basket waterproof by lining with plastic sheet or foil. Working round methodically, fill the basket with roses, beginning at the base and leaving the top of the handle clear. Aim for a natural, tumbling effect as shown below.*

The light crimson R. gallica 'Officinalis', also known as the Apothecary's rose, is the plain mutation of Rosa Mundi.

Try to mix lighter and darker shades of red and pink as much as possible for emphasis and contrast.

The pale mauve rose is 'Fantin-Latour', a beautiful, highly scented tall Centifolia rose.

This arrangement includes many old-fashioned types of rose, including the striped Rosa Mundi.

2 *Drop a block of damp florist foam into the basket. A piece this size will not require taping, but you may need to wedge in smaller pieces of foam to fill in any gaps, depending on the size and shape of the basket.*

3 *Fill the basket with roses, starting at the front edge of one side and working across methodically. The roses at the back should be slightly taller than those at the front of the display.*

Stand the basket on a mat in case moisture leaks onto polished furniture, and top up the foam with a regular spray of water.

4 *The finished basket looks best when viewed from the front, so stand it at any height quite close to a wall or against a background feature.*

Lilac and apricot bouquet

One of the most welcome gifts you can give to anyone is a bunch or posy of flowers, carefully put together and ready to stand in a vase or container of water. If the bouquet includes roses and flowers from your own garden, then the present is even more appreciated. Here, a subtle mixture of lilac, sweet peas and statice is combined with warm apricot roses to make a sweetly scented bunch. The easiest way to make a bouquet like this, whether it is big or small, is to make it in your hand, building it up flower by flower until it is complete and full. Then tie it and finish off with the flourish of a decorative bow in a matching color.

2 First hold one or two stems tightly in one hand and add another flower with the other hand.

At this stage, do not worry that the stems are all different lengths.

Sort out all the flowers you have so that you can see how they look together before bunching them.

1 If the roses are floribunda types, begin by separating them into single stems and clean off the thorns and leaves.

Dividing up a multi-stemmed rose will determine the length of the finished posy.

4 *When the bouquet is finished, cut the stems to make them all the same length and secure the whole thing with a rubber band or wire.*

5 *Lay the bunch of flowers down and wrap a ribbon around the stem, covering the rubber band. Knot the ribbon tightly and tie an attractive bow as a finishing touch.*

3 *Continue adding blooms, mixing the colors and varieties as much as possible and working round evenly. Hold the bunch as tightly as possible.*

Use good-quality ribbon to make the bouquet more of a special gift.

The recipient can remove the ribbon before standing the bouquet in water.

6 *The finished bouquet is pretty enough for a bridesmaid to carry. Try a pink and mauve version instead, or pale yellow mixed with pale blue, or simply white with green foliage.*

101

A beautiful blend of roses and peonies

There is a point in early summer when the old-fashioned shrub roses are in full bloom alongside the extravagant flowers of herbaceous peonies. As both species are multipetaled and are found in a similar range of colors, the two flowers look wonderful mixed together in relaxed arrangements. Although their origins are very different, they both have a very traditional, cottage garden look, best enhanced by simple china containers or old-fashioned pieces, such as this spongeware bowl. This is quite a small arrangement, but depending on how many blooms you are prepared to spare from the garden, you could make it any size you choose.

1 Crumple a square of wire netting so that it fits inside the bowl. You can tape it into place if you wish. Large-headed flowers with stems cut short are top-heavy and therefore need the support of wire in their container.

2 Cut each stem so that it is short enough to slot into the wire and yet leaves the flower head sitting just above the rim.

Use small-scale wire netting from a hardware store or buy special plastic-covered wire from a florist.

Use a peony, such as a double pink 'Sarah Bernhardt'.

3 Begin by putting one flower at a time into the bowl, pushing the stem through the wire mesh. Work carefully round the bowl, keeping the blooms quite tight together.

Mix the different shades of pink and red throughout the arrangement to achieve the maximum contrast.

4 When you have used up all the blooms and the display is finished , give the flowers a light misting of water to keep them fresh.

Peonies and roses will last about the same length of time as cut flowers.

Roses with a full cup shape and rich pink coloring, such as 'Constance Spry', are ideal for this display.

5 The finished arrangement would look good below eye-level on a low occasional table, on a bedside table or as a dining table decoration.

103

Old roses in blue-and-white china

Most of the old-fashioned and shrub roses produce one magnificent flush of flowers in midsummer, often a second flowering later on and occasional blooms throughout the season. When you cut blooms from them, it may seem as though you are wasting many buds that would have flowered later in the season, because the flowers are generally in clusters and their stems are short. However, they are such a pleasure to arrange, and fill the house with so much scent and color, that this is only a small sacrifice. Some varieties can be picked with very short stems for shallow bowls and similar containers. Support the stems with florist foam. The long, curving stems of many of the small-flowered species and hybrid climbing roses may not seem suitable for a vase, but many make lovely, if short-lived, displays.

2 *Choose compatible containers in a range of shapes and sizes. Divide the roses into different types and put each type in a separate container.*

1 *Recut the stem at an angle and cut off and clear away any of the lower foliage and thorns that will be below the water level in the container.*

A jug of climbing roses

Cut flowering stems off the very long trailing laterals of rambler roses, such as this 'Seagull'. Snip away faded flowers, the lower stems and foliage. A tall jug with a narrow neck keeps stems in place, but allows flowers to spread naturally.

Rosa gallica 'Officinalis' has light crimson petals, golden stamens and typical tough gallica foliage.

4 Position the three small arrangements, with the tallest at the back. Leave enough space around them so that each is clear to see, but together they make a harmonious single group.

Old garden roses

Red/purple
Tuscany Superb
Charles de Mills
Baron Girod de L'Ain
Reine de Violettes
Mme. Isaac Perreire

Pink
Comte de Chambord
Petite de Hollande
Celestial
Fantin-Latour
Queen of Denmark
Louise Odier
Reine Victoria

White
Boule de Neige
Comtesse de Murinais
Shailer's White Moss
Blanchefleur
Mme. Hardy

3 Place the second variety in a different container. Keep the roses with the longest stems for the tallest jug or vase.

The pretty buds and strong green foliage of this 'Président de Sèze' add extra interest.

'Ferdinand Pichard', a fine striped rose, has neat, organized flowers and is repeat flowering.

Use crumpled wire or florist foam if the roses are difficult to arrange in a bowl of this shape.

Yellow roses in a pink glazed bowl

Traditionally, the classic rose bowl for displaying perfect roses is round and quite shallow, with a gently curving outline. However, it is not always easy to support roses with heavy heads in a bowl of this shape, and you will have to find a method of holding each stem in place away from its immediate neighbor. Some rose bowls have an integral wire mesh disc on top of the rim, but a simpler and cheaper solution is to use any favorite bowl of the right shape and to add your own crumpled chicken wire or plastic-coated wire netting. Mix in another type of flower or foliage to conceal the wire mesh below and to provide a contrasting background to set off the color and shape of the blooms. Here, bright acid green *Alchemilla mollis* complements rich yellow 'Graham Thomas' roses.

2 Squeeze the wire a little so that it drops easily into the bowl and rests about halfway down. If it does not feel secure, attach it firmly to the inside of the bowl with florist's tape.

Plastic-coated wire lasts well and does not damage precious china, glass or metal containers.

1 Begin by cutting out a rough circle of small- to medium-sized wire netting with wire cutters. Make the circle slightly larger than the area of the top of the bowl.

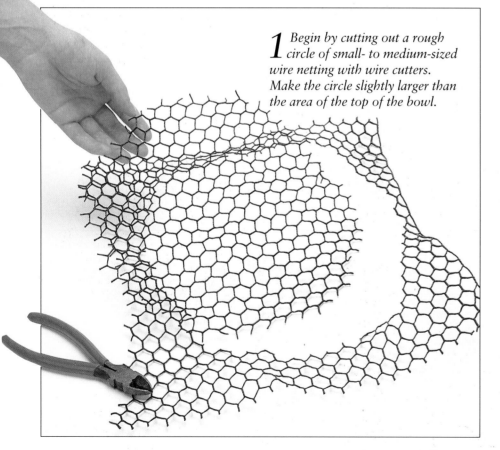

3 Add sprays of Alchemilla *to the bowl, covering the wire completely and creating a soft, curving outline. The* Alchemilla *can extend beyond the edge of the bowl to make a wide, low display.*

4 Space the roses evenly throughout *the arrangement, inbetween the foliage. Leave the center stems a little longer than those around the lower edge. Give a fine mist of water.*

'Graham Thomas' is a good *choice of rose as a cut flower, as it keeps its color well and has pretty cup-shaped blooms.*

5 This arrangement would look *good as the centerpiece of a large dining table or on a low table where it can be viewed from above.*

The pink, sponged glaze on this 1950s bowl is an effective *foil to the green and yellow flowers.*

A creative approach

A flower arrangement need not be confined to a conventional vase or container and roses do not have to be stood in water in the traditional way. Since floral foam can be the means of providing both water and support to flowers, there is no end to the creative possibilities this offers. All kinds of objects can become the container for a display or you could dispense with one altogether and make a free-form arrangement. A brief search through the average house will produce dozens of different items that can become containers or the starting point for a spectacular display. Roses are easy and amenable flowers, they can be cut short or used full length and are relatively long-lived as cut flowers. They are ideal to use for a wide variety of decorations and their adaptability, strong stems and sturdy heads make them the perfect choice for everything from garlands to table decorations.

A traditional wreath of striped roses

Garlands or wreaths are a good way of making the most of a few special flowers. They have lost their old image of only being hung on a door at Christmas and are used decoratively throughout the year for any special occasion or they can be laid flat as a table centerpiece. The traditional method of making them used a wire and damp moss base with the flowers wired on, but these days the easiest way is to use a ready-made foam ring. Roses are ideal as flowers to use in wreaths and garlands along with some other foliage or plant material to work as a filler. You could, of course, make a very beautiful and luxurious wreath with just roses, but a filler of some kind is useful for covering the foam completely and adding contrast to the flowers. A wreath made in this way on a damp foam base will last for several days, especially if you keep it moist with an occasional fine spray of water.

You will need a loop of wire if you intend to hang the wreath vertically.

Follow the maker's instructions on soaking the foam so that it is neither too wet nor too dry.

2 *Using short stems of gypsophila as a filler, work around the ring, covering it completely.*

3 *Next, begin to add short stems of dianthus, spacing them evenly throughout the gypsophila.*

4 *Add the roses, filling the spaces between the dianthus to create a densely textured effect.*

1 *Make a small loop around the ring with some garden wire. Then soak the ring in water before filling it with flowers. Work with the ring held vertically or horizontally, whichever is comfortable for you.*

Candlesticks adorned with miniature roses

Roses always look good used as table decorations, and partnered with candlelight they look even better. Here, two very ordinary recycled glass candlesticks have been given a glamorous treatment with a clever ring of foam around them to hold small red roses and sprigs of fern leaf. The idea can be adapted for any type of candlestick as the candles in effect hold everything in place. Just be sure to make the foam ring big enough to hold the stems securely and do not let the candles burn right down too near to the flowers. Any small-flowered rose or miniature rose will be suitable for this arrangement and ivy leaves could replace the fern if you prefer. Colorful candles look good as a contrast to the flowers, or choose plain cream or white ones for a more classic look.

1 Cut small pieces of foam about 1in(2.5cm) thick. Then make a hole right through the foam by pushing down with the candle.

2 Mark out a circle around the hole, about 3.5in(9cm) across, depending on size of candles and holder. Cut it out with a sharp knife and soak the foam.

3 Prepare the roses and foliage by separating the flowers from the bunches and cutting the stems short. Do the same with the foliage.

You can pull apart a stem of leather fern into several small leaves.

4 Place the foam ring on the candlestick and push the candle through. Use small pieces of florist fixing tape to secure it if necessary.

5 Once you have a basis of green foliage all over the foam, begin to add the roses and buds, working methodically around the ring.

6 The finished decoration could be a matching pair of candlesticks or a single decoration. One for each guest would look pretty on a table setting.

Put the foliage in place as a filler and to provide a contrast to the flowers.

Most candlesticks have a suitable 'drip tray' on which you can support the foam ring.

This small red rose looks pretty in bud and when it has opened out. Use of a mixture of buds and open flowers in the arrangement for maximum interest.

Roses, scabious and cornflower table decoration

1 *Cut a piece of foam to the right thickness for the dish then mark out a circle by pressing a round object onto the foam. Cut the foam to shape using a sharp kitchen knife.*

2 *Wet the foam as usual and push it onto a pin holder, as here, or use a special foam holder. An old-fashioned pin holder is good and heavy. A foam holder will need to be taped in place.*

Some people simply cannot bring themselves to cut a rose with a very short stem. However, once you have come to terms with the idea, you can begin to make all kinds of unexpected and unusual decorations and arrangements in a variety of containers. The flower heads become a means of creating color and texture to make things such as table decorations. You will need a suitable container and this can either be part of the overall arrangement or simply a tray or base that is hidden by the display but holds the water and florist foam. In the example shown here, a blue-and-white china soup plate makes the perfect container, providing an area deep enough to hold the foam, but pretty enough to make an edging to the finished display, which in turn becomes part of the table decoration.

3 *Position the damp foam in the center of the plate and cut all the flowers short, so that the stems are only about 2in(5cm) long. Put the first rose in place in the center.*

Arrange a ring of cornflowers right around the central rose.

4 *Make a ring of scabious flowers outside the cornflowers, pushing the stems into the foam to secure them. The delicate mauve of these blooms tones pleasingly with the bright blue of the cornflowers.*

Arrange the flowers as close as possible to each other without squashing them.

Variations on a theme

In the arrangement featured here, the central rose is a deep pink 'Madame Isaac Perreire' and the paler roses around the edge are 'Celestial', a beautiful alba rose. You could completely change the look of this display by choosing different colors. Try a deep yellow central rose with the same mauve and blue flowers in between and a paler creamy yellow rose around the edge. Or you could try a very deep purplish-red central rose, again surrounded by rings of mauve and blue flowers, and alternate crimson and pink roses for the outside ring. Alternatively, you could achieve a totally different look with all white roses and soft greeny gray foliage or flowers between the two rings

5 *Finish with a final ring, this time of roses, which simply sit inside the rim of the dish. Top up the dish with water for the roses and to keep the foam damp.*

Tea cups and a rosy hat

A very simple but effective way of using garden roses is to line up a row of three, four or five cups and saucers and use them as small vases to hold single blooms or little bunches of your favorite roses. You could choose cups all in shades of pink or with a rose-decorated theme, or you might prefer plain white cups or pale green ones, which would look equally pretty. The finished group can stand in a line along a shelf or on a windowsill or down the center of a table. On a small round table they might look better grouped closer together. Here we also look at how to decorate a summer hat with a few special roses for a grand occasion.

1 *Choose an attractive group of cups and saucers and fill them with water. Select appropriate roses for each cup.*

Cut stems to the right length and remove any unwanted foliage.

Split the stems from the base upwards to help the roses take up water.

2 *Make small arrangements in each cup, adding a few pieces of foliage to one or two if you wish. You can mix different varieties or keep to a single type.*

A hatful of roses

This is 'Aloha', a climbing rose with an old-fashioned look and beautiful rich color.

1 *Choose two perfect matching blooms and trim, leaving about 3in(7.5cm) of stem and leaf. Wrap tape around the stem, making sure that you enclose the cut end.*

3 *Arrange the cups, balancing light and dark flowers throughout the line and mixing solid color cups with lighter, floral sprigged ones.*

Reine des Violettes

3 Using fine rose wire, attach the rose stems to the hat by threading the wire right through the straw inside the crown and out again. Twist the wire tightly round the stems a few times and neatly cut off any extra wire.

4 Fold a chiffon scarf around the base of the crown or wrap a wide ribbon round it to cover the rose stems. Knot or tie into a bow at the back of the hat.

2 Put the two roses together, one just above the other and bind them together with tape to make one stem. Position the roses on the hat at the base of the crown at one side.

'Celestial' has very pretty grayish green foliage that sets off its pale pink flowers very well.

Rose 'Félicité Parmentier'

Rose 'Fantin-Latour'

Rose 'Président de Sèze'

The deep, glowing purple-red of the gallica rose 'Charles de Mills' matches this charming Victorian tea cup.

Roses in clear glass

Sometimes you need to make a table decoration or arrangement for a room quickly and nothing could be faster to put together than these two ideas. Both rely on sparkling clean and shiny glass, so the first thing to do is to spend a couple of minutes buffing the glass until it glitters. Pour the water in carefully, in order not to splash the sides and create tide marks and spots on the glass. Economical with flowers as well as time, these ideas are the perfect way to achieve real impact with very little effort. For a different effect, float single flowers on small individual glass dishes or glasses for a very pretty table setting for a special meal.

Choose a rose variety that has plenty of interest inside the flower, either with lots of petals like this one or with a pretty center and stamens.

Cut the stem away from the rose head at the point where the stem fattens out into the flower.

1 *Decide how many blooms you have room for in your container and prepare each rose the same way. A good solid rose such as 'Graham Thomas' is best for this treatment.*

2 *The water should be just deep enough to allow the flowers to float easily. Lay the bloom very gently on the surface, so that the flower head does not become too waterlogged.*

Bottled roses

On a hot night, you could add a few ice cubes to the water or perhaps a few drops of rose essential oil for added fragrance.

Adjust the level of the water according to the height of the bowl and the angle from which it will be seen.

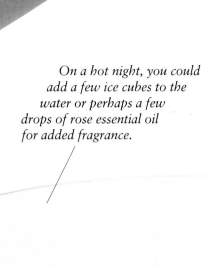

1 Choose two bottles that relate in shape but vary in height. Fill with water. Leave a long stem on one rose but trim away lower leaves.

2 Stand the first rose in a tall bottle and then put the second rose in the smaller bottle. Adjust the height of the roses if necessary.

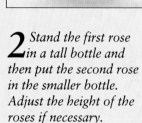

3 Stand the bottles in their final position, one in front of the other. Turn the roses so that they face forwards but do not cross each other.

'Graham Thomas' is one of the new breed of English roses, old-fashioned in style, but repeat-flowering.

3 Continue adding blooms. The final number will depend on the size of the bowl, but there should be enough room so that they do not all crowd each other but can float freely.

Layered pot pourri and little pots

Another way to exploit the decorative possibilities of dried roses is to layer up pot pourri mixtures in a plain glass tank and decorate the top surface with whole dried roses. As we have seen, garden-grown roses dry very well and retain their color and scent better than many commercially produced varieties. (For more information on drying roses, see pages 78-79.) The petal mixture can be simply decorative or you can make a proper pot pourri with essential oils and fixatives. Divide the different colored layers with sticks of cinnamon, large dried leaves or any other material that seems suitable. You can make the color scheme as bold or as subtle as you like. The texture of dried roses looks superb when combined with old terracotta. Fill small flower pots with a mass of rose heads and decorate them with a jaunty ribbon. The deep purplish red rose featured here is 'Zigeunerknabe' ('Gypsy Boy').

Little pots with tartan bows

Fill small pots with dried florist foam. Disguise it with dry moss secured with small wire loops. Cover surface completely with wired dried roses.

1 Put a layer of pot pourri at the bottom of the glass tank and press it down well. With care, you can position the best pieces and prettiest flowers against the front of the glass.

This mixture is a home-made pot pourri of roses and other dried garden flowers and leaves, including tulip petals, hibiscus and peony petals.

2 Cover the first layer of pot pourri with some dried leaves, such as eucalyptus, to create a barrier between the first and second layers. Then put in a row of cinnamon sticks to cover the leaves.

Eucalyptus leaves provide an interesting contrast and divide up the different layers.

Cinnamon sticks also add another scent to the display.

4 *The finished arrangement is ideal as a bedroom decoration. Stand it away from direct bright sunlight; it causes the colors to fade quickly.*

Above: *Add bows or leave pots plain. This bow has been glued directly to the pot. Make several pots the same or stand pairs on shelves and tables.*

3 *Add another layer of a different color pot pourri and then decorate the whole of the top with complete dried rose heads from side to side.*

121

Index to Roses

Page numbers in normal type refer to entries in the main text; page numbers in *italics* refer to entries in panels, captions and annotations.

Credits

The majority of the photographs featured in this book have been taken by Neil Sutherland and are © Colour Library Books. The publishers wish to thank the following photographers for providing additional photographs, credited here by page number and position on the page (BL: Bottom left, TR: Top right, etc.).

Biofotos (Heather Angel): 12(B), 16-17(T), 20(B), 44-5(C)
Gillian Beckett: 33(BR), 37(BR)
Eric Crichton: 8, 10, 12(TL), 17(BR), 18(B), 19(T), 22(B), 23(TL), 26(BL), 27(BL), 29(TL,BR), 41(BR)
John Glover: 17(T), 32, 33(R), 38-9(T), 54(B)
Pamela Harper: 27(R)
Jerry Harpur: 5, 12(TR), 46(BL)
S & O Mathews Photography: 14(BL), 17(BL), 20(TR), 58(T)
John Mattock: 14-15(B), 43(TL)
Natural Image:
Robin Fletcher: 22-3(BC)
Bob Gibbons: 13(T), 14(T), 15(T,B), 61(CL)
Peter Wilson: 61(TL,BR)
Photos Horticultural (Michael & Lois Warren): 18(T), 20-1(C), 21(T), 23(R), 26-7(C), 28-9(C), 29(TR), 48(BL), 52(BL), 61(C,CB)
Harry Smith Photographic Collection: 13(B), 16-17(B), 18-19(B), 30(BL), 59(TL)

Acknowledgements

John Mattock would like to acknowledge the constructive and valuable help of the Secretary and Staff of The Royal National Rose Society, St. Albans, Hertfordshire; Dickson's Nurseries, Newtownards, Northern Ireland; Harkness New Roses, Hitchin, Hertfordshire; W. Kordes Söhne, Sparrieshoop, Germany; Edmund's Roses, Wilsonville, Oregon; Conard Pyle (Star Roses) Co., West Grove, Pennsylvania; Beverly Dobson, Irvington, New York.